WHERE TO GO
IN
YUGOSLAVIA

HAROLD DENNIS-JONES

THOMSON HOLIDAYS

SETTLE PRESS

HIPPOCRENE BOOKS INC.

Texts and maps © 1989 Harold Dennis-Jones
Maps designed and executed by Harold Dennis-
Jones with help from Cathy Sumner
All rights reserved. No part of this publication
may be reproduced or transmitted in any form or
by any means without permission.
First published by Settle Press
32 Savile Row
London W1X 1AG

ISBN (Paperback) 0 907070 56 6

Published in USA by
Hippocrene Books Inc
171 Madison Avenue, New York

ISBN 0-87052-722-3

Printed by Villiers Publications Ltd
26a Shepherds Hill, London N6 5AH

Contents

WHERE TO GO IN YUGOSLAVIA

Chapter One:	The Appeal of Yugoslavia	5
Chapter Two:	Which Resort?	8
Chapter Three:	Choosing Your Holiday	12

THE COAST

Chapter Four:	Istria	15
Chapter Five:	The Gulf of Kvarner	28
Chapter Six:	Northern Dalmatia	36
Chapter Seven:	Central Dalmatia	46
Chapter Eight:	Southern Dalmatia	63
Chapter Nine:	The Coast of Montenegro	78

THE INLAND AREAS

Chapter Ten:	Slovenia and the Yugoslav Alps	87
Chapter Eleven:	Inland Croatia	91
Chapter Twelve:	Northern Serbia and the Vojvodina	95
Chapter Thirteen:	Southern Serbia and Kosovo	103
Chapter Fourteen:	Macedonia	108
Chapter Fifteen:	Inland Montenegro	113
Chapter Sixteen:	Bosnia-Herzegovina	116

GENERAL INFORMATION

Chapter Seventeen:	The Background to Your Visit	123
Chapter Eighteen:	Practical Information	132
Chapter Nineteen:	A Look at the Language(s)	139

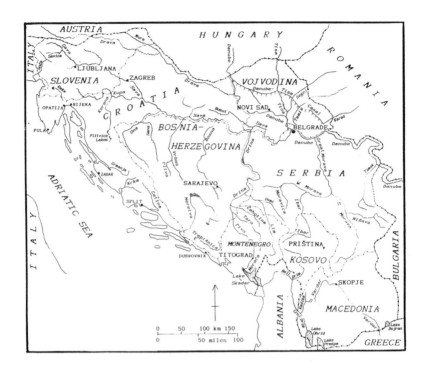

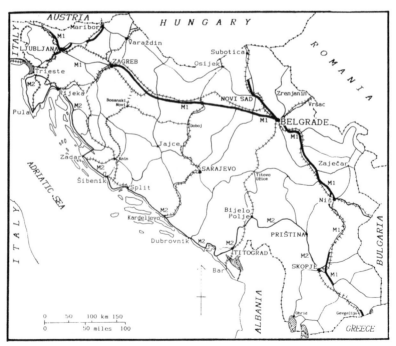

Chapter One

The Appeal of Yugoslavia

Yugoslavia's coast is widely recognised as one of Europe's outstanding holiday areas. Its scenery's magnificent, its climate superb. Its clear bright sunshine and clean seas make a very welcome change from the murk and pollution of so many Western cities. There's an awful lot of Yugoslav coast, too. If you include its hundreds of offshore islands it winds for 4000 rocky, indented miles all the way from the Italian frontier at Trieste to Albania.

It gives you a choice of well over 100 resorts of every sort and size. Its modern accommodation includes mostly very recently built self-catering blocks and is well calculated to suit all ages and tastes. Some resorts are based on tiny peninsula towns and villages, others on ancient fishing harbours nestling in quiet bays. Some lie close to spectacular stone-built fortified towns whose walls date back to medieval days and sometimes beyond. Others stand completely on their own, often in vast pine-covered areas. Some are quiet and remote. Some are decidedly lively. Some cater specially for all-age families, and some for young children.

Exciting excursions are possible from most of them, including some to superb old Turkish towns or Eastern Orthodox monasteries unlike anything we know in our Western world, and some to areas of superb scenery and fascinating wildlife.

Yet Yugoslavia's far more varied and complex than the rest of the world realises. Despite all the development that has taken place on the coast and its islands there's a surprising lot there that's still little known. The mainland and the 66 inhabited islands can still boast lots of quiet corners as well as flourishing resorts. Remote hamlets still exist where each house owns its own well and communal services like telephones and electricity are unknown and roads totally absent. There are tiny harbours where strangers – even Yugoslav strangers – rarely appear.

Over 700 islands shelter this coast and help make the sailing excellent. Fishing's decidedly good too. Some of the scenery's among Europe's most striking and most unusual. And underwater swimmers can revel in magnificently coloured marine creatures and corals. It can be a holiday paradise.

The country's inland areas are totally different. But they're equally attractive. Three-quarters of Yugoslavia consists of mountains. Large areas are snow-covered for up to six months of the year and the winter sports potential is enormous. All year the mountains' scenery is magnificent. Many regions offer excellent summer walking. In addition, one-third of the country's covered by forests where the wildlife's unbelievably varied. It includes even lynx, wolf, and bear, as well as a vast variety of flora and opportunities for first-rate birdwatching.

Yugoslavia's above-ground rivers have a total length of over 74,000 miles. That includes the Drava's entire 600-odd miles from its source in the Alps to where it joins the Danube, as well as some 370 miles of the mighty Danube itself and 200 miles or so of the Tisa, itself longer and larger than the Rhine. Of the 40-odd rivers named on our frontispiece map over 30 flow through spectacular gorges, one of which is second in depth only to the USA's Grand Canyon. On top of that Yugoslavia's karst regions include some of the world's largest underground rivers. You can actually visit one that has cut a 400-foot-high gorge in underground limestone.

Some 15 areas, including one island region, have been declared National Parks. Even the two whose interest is mainly historical offer stupendous scenery.

Canoeing and fishing on the country's rivers can be superb. Of its 300 lakes some are perched high on mountainsides in or close to notable National Parks or nature reserves. One of federal Yugoslavia's constituent areas, the largely flat Autonomous Province of the Vojvodina, alone offers over 1000 miles of rivers, lakes, and vast canals suitable for sailing, canoeing, fishing, and watersports.

Dotted about among all this you'll find an amazing variety of towns and villages. Two sizeable coastal settlements still make everyday use of surviving Roman buildings. Lovely little towns built in imitation of Venice are scattered almost all the way along the coast. Inland you'll find towns and villages almost purely Turkish in character. They're the result of 400 years of Turkish rule. There are Alpine towns and villages in the north. In the south they can be Macedonian. In between they may be largely Austrian, Hungarian, Romanian, or decidedly modern European, to say nothing of various more localised styles.

The ancient Orthodox monasteries scattered mainly through the country's southern half deserve special mention. They began to be known to Westerners only after occupying Turks were forced to leave the country between 1878 and 1912. They're little known even today, except to a very few specialist art historians. Yet the magnificent frescos painted on their churches' walls represent one of the world's outstanding treasuries of historical art. The paintings go back to the 12th century.

Two of these monasteries, four of Yugoslavia's ancient towns, two of its National Parks, and one underground river's cave system have been included in UNESCO's worldwide list of some 160 natural and artistic sites of importance to all of us. That perhaps gives some idea of what the country can offer – quite apart from its magnificent and already much-appreciated coastline.

It's the coast however that attracts the great bulk of Yugoslavia's holidaymakers. It's natural, then, that this book should start by concentrating on the coast and telling people what there is to enjoy there. After that we outline the other things that Yugoslavia can offer. The choice is so vast that not a lot of detail's possible in a book of this length, particularly when the country's history, art, architecture, wildlife, traditions, and even its language and way of life are so little known to us in the West.

Even its geography's unfamiliar. Our maps concentrate on basic information. They show through roads (which are surfaced, of course). Also those railway routes over which the excellent new "Inter-City" trains or international rolling stock operates. We hope that they too will help you enjoy your holiday and make you want to see more of Yugoslavia.

Chapter Two

Which Resort?

Resorts are classified according to what you'll feel is the size of the town or tourist settlement you visit, not according to objective data such as population, etc. L = large, M = medium, S = small, T = tiny, and I = isolated – usually because the hotel or tourist settlement's right on its own.

Distances to the town or village the resort's attached to are defined in minutes' walk (W) or miles (M); hotels may also be right in the middle of a town or village (Mi), or under 10 minutes' walk at its edge (E), or isolated (I) if there isn't any town or village nearby.

Beaches may be sandy (Sa), shingly (Sh), rocky (R), pebbly (P), or cemented (C), or a mixture of any of these.

Excursions may be excellent in quantity and quality (E), or good (G), or moderate (M), or restricted (R) – the latter usually because the resort or hotel is remote or isolated.

Handicapped holidaymakers should note that nearly all Yugoslav seaside hotels are built on steep or steepish slopes that can involve a fair number of steps. Enquire before you book.

	Size	Distance	Beach	Outings
Istria				
Ankaran	T	E	Sh	M
Piran	S	M	C	E
Portorož	L	M	Sa/Sh	E
Umag	M	½–1½M	Sa/Sh	G
Novigrad Istra	M	E	P	G
Poreč town	M	Mi	C	G
– Lanterna	M	8M	P	G
– Červar	M	6M	P/R	G
– Materada	M	5M	R/P	G
– Spadiči	M	2M	R/P	G
– Pical	M	1M	R/P	G
– Brulo	M	2M	R/P	G
– Plava Laguna	M	2½M	R/Sh	G
– Zelena Laguna	M	3M	R/Sh	G
Funtana	T	Mi	R/P	G
Vrsar	S	E	R/P	G
Koversada	M	Mi	R/P	G

	Size	Distance	Beach	Outings
Rovinj mainland	M	Mi/E	R/P	G
– islands	T	I	R/P	G
Veliki Brion	T	I	R/Sh	G
Pula town	L	Mi	–	G
– Zlatne Stijene	L	2M	R	G
– Verudela	L	3M	R	G
– Medulin	L	7M	P	G
Rabac	M	E	Sh/P	G
Moščenička Draga	S	Mi	P	G
Medveja	S	Mi	R	G
Lovran	M	Mi	R	G
Opatija	L	Mi	R	E

Gulf of Kvarner

	Size	Distance	Beach	Outings
Kraljevica	M	Mi	R	G
Crikvenica	L	Mi	Sh/Sa	E
Selce	M	Mi	Sh/Sa	E
Novi Vinodolski	M	Mi	Sa	E
Starigrad Paklenica	T	E	R	G
Cres	S	E	R/P	M
Mali Lošinj	S	E	R/P	M
Krk town	S	E	R	M
Punat	S	E	R	M
Baška	S	E	R	M
Malinska	S	E	R	M
Njivice	S	E	R/C	M
Omišalj	S	E	R/P	M
Rab town	M	E	R/C	M
Lopar	T	Mi	Sa	M
Supetarska Draga	T	Mi	Sh	M

Northern Dalmatia

	Size	Distance	Beach	Outings
Pag	S	Mi	R/P	M
Zaton	S	E	Sa	M
Petrčane	S	E	R/Sh	M
Zadar town	M	E	P/Sh/C	G
– Borik	M	Mi	P/Sh/C	G
Filipjakov	T	E	R	M
Biograd na moru	S	E	R/Sh	G
Crvena Luka	T	I	Sa	G
Pakoštane	T	I	Sa	G
Pirovac	S	E	R/P	G
Vodice	S	E/10W	P	G
Šibenik town	M	Mi/20W	R/C	G
– Solaris	M	I	P/Sh	E
Zlarin	T	E	R/P	R

	Size	Distance	Beach	Outings
Božava	T	E	R/P	R
Kornat islands	I	I	R	–
Murter	S	Mi	R/P	M

Central Dalmatia

	Size	Distance	Beach	Outings
Primošten	S	E	R/P	M
Rogoznica	S	E	R/P	M
Trogir (Medena)	M	3M	R/P	G
Kaštel Stari	M	Mi	R/P	G
Split town	L	Mi	R/C	E
– Hotel Lav	M	5M	P	E
Omiš	M	Mi	Sh/Sa	G
Brela	S	Mi	Sh/P	G
Baška Voda	S	Mi	Sh/P	G
Makarska	M	E/Mi	P	G
Tučepi	M	Mi	P	E
Podgora	S	E	R/P	G
Igrane	S	E	R/P	G
Žigovošče	S	E	P	G
Zaostrog	T	E	P	M
Gradac na moru	S	E	P	M
Supetar	S	E	P	M
Postira	S	E	P	M
Bol	S	E	P	M
Hvar town	M	E	R	G
Starigrad na Hvaru	S	15W	P/R/C	M
Vrboska	S	30W	R/P	M
Jelsa	S	15W	R/P	M

Southern Dalmatia

	Size	Distance	Beach	Outings
Neum-Klek	S	E	P	M
Orebić	M	15W	R/P/Sa	G
Korčula town	M	15W	R/P	G
Vela Luka	S	E	R	M
Lumbarda	S	E	R/P	M
Brna	T	E	R/Sa	M
Slano	T	Mi	P	G
Orašac	T	Mi	R	G
Mljet	I	I	R	R
Šipanska Luka	S	E	R/P	M
Lopud town	S	E	P/Sh/Sa	M
Koločep	T	E	Sa	M
Dubrovnik				
– Dubrava/Babin Kuk	L	4M	R/P	E
– Lapad area	L	3M	R/Sh	E
– Gruž area	L	1½M	R	E

10

	Size	Distance	Beach	Outings
– Danče Bay and Pile	L	½–1M	R/Sh	E
– Ploče area	L	1M	R/Sh	E
– Kupari	M	4M	P	E
– Srebreno	M	4M	P/Sa	E
– Mlini	M	4½M	P	E
Plat	M	I	P	E
Cavtat	M	E/10W	R/P	E

The Coast of Montenegro

	Size	Distance	Beach	Outings
Hercegnovi	M	E/15W	R/P	G
Risan	T	E	R/P	M
Kotor	M	E	R	M
Budva town	M	10W	P	G
– Slovenska Plaža	I	20W	P/Sh	G
Bečiči	I	I	P/Sa	G
Miločer	S	I	Sh/Sa	G
Sveti Stefan mainland	S	I	Sh/Sa	G
Sveti Stefan island	S	I	Sh/Sa	G
Petrovac	S	E–1M	P/Sh/Sa	G
Sutomore	S	E	P/Sa	G
Ulcinj	M	E	Sa	G

Personal choices

Large and lively (older towns) – Portorož, Opatija, Dubrovnik; (new tourist settlements) - Zelena Laguna.

Friendly and colourful - Cavtat.

For children - Lopar and Ulcinj for sand; Slovenska Plaža for modern facilities.

Away from it all - Mljet, Kornat National Park.

Multi-generation families - Cavtat, Funtana.

Luxurious setting - Sveti Stefan.

Spectacular setting - Risan.

For younger folk sampling Yugoslavia - Hotel Parentino in Poreč, Hotel Dubravka in Dubrovnik.

For senior citizens relaxing in the off-season - Hotel Mlini at Mlini.

Inland ideas

Slovenia's Alpine resorts can all be recommended both for non-spectacular winter skiing and for summer walking. Ohrid makes a fine summer lakeside resort, especially for anyone interested also in the town's astonishing historical connections. Plitvice, Durmitor, and the other National Park resorts all offer good walking and plenty of nature and wildlife interest. Art-lovers will be bowled over by a tour of the most important monasteries.

Chapter Three

Choosing Your Holiday

If you want to enjoy your Yugoslav holiday to the full it's worth spending time thinking about the varied possibilities.

Package tour . . . ?

The advantages of packages are obvious. You pay less than independent travellers, you pay it all in one go. You have people around who provide help and information and, above all, are on hand should anything go seriously wrong. The firm you book with also usually organises excursions to places of interest and evening entertainments – barbecues, fish picnics, and the like – which you can join without the hassle of queuing for bus or ferry tickets or in other time-consuming spots. Given Yugoslavia's language problems, all this represents considerable benefits. Except in places where English speakers are normally found – hotels, tourist information offices, and the like – relatively few people speak your language.

Packages come in various types. On the coast you can opt for hotel accommodation if you wish and have all your meals in your hotel. Or you can choose bed and breakfast and half-board – a meal in the evening while you eat out in the middle of the day. You've a vast range of accommodation choices, from really luxurious to pleasantly modest.

Self-catering apartments are also now very widely available on the coast, and virtually always have supermarkets located close by where you can buy all your food. You hardly need words in a supermarket, so shopping's easy. If you do have to say something, a few words of basic German can help. Because German visitors predominate on the coast almost everyone dealing with them there scuttles into German when difficulties loom.

Beach holidays however aren't all that's available. Packages cover also skiing, mountain walking, mountain lakeside holidays, wildlife (in some of the country's superb National Parks), schooner tours, "flotilla" sailing, bareboat charter (for sail or powered craft), sea fishing, coach touring, art tours with specialist guides, and "desert island" holidays that are the nearest thing you can get to being genuinely "away from it all" without losing the basic amenities.

On these last, you may have to pump water from your own well. You'll depend on bottle gas for your cooking, lighting, and fridge, and on the twice-weekly provision boat for the food and drink you order. Your accommodation will be fairly simple (a modernised stone cottage). But the setting will genuinely be like nowhere else in the world.

The schooner tours also deserve a special note. Space on the boats may be limited. Not every cabin will necessarily have its own shower and loo. Sails and rigging are largely decorative. But the boats are genuine old trading schooners that their owners couldn't bear to see broken up. They let you see the coast in all its beauty and all its glory – tiny villages, fantastic island scenery, staggeringly lovely towns, with fishing, surfboarding, and endless trips ashore. A fortnight's figure-of-eight trip, based on Split, takes in the whole of Dalmatia. Younger folk, in particular, rave about these trips.

Art tours and other inland holidays are still relatively specialised. Yugoslavia was a poverty-stricken, largely illiterate country 50 years ago. Its enormous store of treasures is still waiting to be discovered – and no one's keener on preserving and displaying them than the Yugoslavs themselves, poor though the country still is compared with our prosperous West. The possibilities are staggering.

If you buy a package tour that aims to introduce you to any of these delights you can reasonably expect your guides to be decently (or extremely) knowledgeable.

... or on your own?

What happens if you want to explore Yugoslavia on your own? There's nothing to stop you going exactly where you want in your own boat, your own car, a hired car, or by public plane, train, or bus. Restrictions are minimal – one or two naval areas closed to non-Yugoslav persons, a very few military areas (including airports) where photography's forbidden, and that's about the lot.

What's sometimes difficult is getting accurate information – especially in advance. The Yugoslav National Tourist Office in London (or New York, etc) is your obvious first port-of-call. But they won't necessarily be able to produce immediately even a full list of hotels, nor an up-to-date railway timetable, let alone exact details of the more variable ferry routes to all the islands. What they can do is tell you where to write (or phone) for fuller information. Letters to Yugoslavs don't necessarily produce replies – prompt or otherwise. Phoning may help.

So – start months in advance, and badger everyone till you've got everything you want. Be studiously polite, of course. When you feel you've made so much nuisance of yourself that no one will want to see you, you'll find you're given an overpowering welcome when you finally show up. And you'll have a wonderful time – apart from occasional battles for information. This isn't some perversity of character in the Yugoslavs. They just don't think life's long enough to get themselves as steamed up as we too often do. "No problem", they say (and they say it so often you'll sometimes want to scream), "Sit down and have a drink".

One bit of information you'll find essential if you're touring is good maps. This is dealt with in Chapter 18 (Motoring). Ideally, you'll also need books giving infinitely more detail about your chosen area or subject than can be provided in a book of this length. That's dealt with in the same chapter (under Further Reading).

If you buy a simple package and want to explore seriously, say, some nearby town or area, your tour operator's rep should be able to tell you where to hire a car (if one's really necessary) or help you find a taxi driver who speaks English and agree a charge for the day or whatever (prices are usually extremely reasonable).

What's more, in every region people exist who are extraordinarily knowledgeable on everything connected with it. Architecture, traditions, history, wildlife – you name it. With luck, you'll even discover someone like this who speaks English or some language you can cope with. Just keep asking, starting with your guide – and don't be shy about. it. The Yugoslavs are delighted with people who are interested. But they don't always know how to bring their knowledge to your notice.

When to go

There's considerable difference between the weather inland and on the coast. Deep inland – in Belgrade, Zagreb, Sarajevo, Skopje, and the regions round them – temperatures rise steeply from about mid-April on, reaching *averages* of over 80°F in the heat of the day throughout July and August (that means some days can be a lot hotter). From late April till mid- or late September you can reckon on 70°F in early afternoon. Evenings are always much cooler. And winters can be downright bitter. The average minimum temperature in Belgrade, for instance, drops to freezing in December and well below in January and February.

The coast has a similar, but less extreme, pattern. Low-season January and February are the coldest months, not improved in some areas by the occasional cold northerly "bora" wind coming down from the Alps (some remain pleasantly warm, however). But even night temperatures hover around 40°F, and the daytime high is some 9 or 10 degrees above that. Peak-season July and August are hot

– but the average maximum is below rather than above 80°F.

Shoulder months can be very pleasant indeed. April can be springlike and May pleasantly warm, while June is as hot as many will want. September and even October are often delightful, and sometimes warm enough for bougainvilleas whose colours have been a delight through the late spring and summer to bloom a second time.

All Yugoslavia's on holiday in August, and so is the rest of Europe. The coast in particular becomes extremely congested. You'll be alright once you've made your bookings. But you'll notice the difference when you start to move around. Avoid August if you can.

Rainfall all the year is light, with the peak (such as it is) coming in November and December in Split at the coast's midpoint, and in May and June in Belgrade. Occasional ferocious thunderstorms descend on the coast in summer, thanks to the "jugo" southern wind blowing off the Egyptian desert. But you're no sooner wet through than you're dry again as the sun comes out.

While this is the general picture, there can be regional variations. Mountain areas, plentiful in Yugoslavia, are obviously colder than lower-lying land, and in summer even richer in burning ultra-violet rays. There are other variations. The little pocket of Croatia, for instance, between Karlovac, southwest of Zagreb, and the sea, usually escapes excessive summer heat, thanks to mild mountain breezes. And in recent years the weather hasn't always behaved as expected. But that's the case worldwide.

THE COAST

Chapter Four

Istria

Istria (Istra to Yugoslavs) is the triangular peninsula at the coast's northernmost point. It's different from coastal stretches further south. No gaunt, bare, mountain ridges flank the coast, sweeping steeply down to the water's edge. Hills are plentiful inland. But most of the terrain's less starkly mountainous. Much of the land in fact is fertile red soil and well-cultivated. Woods of various species cover many crags and slopes bordering the sea. There are endless bays of varying size and shape. Little coastal towns hide in sheltered inlets or perch for protection on peninsulas once ringed by walls. Lots of older inland settlements are also planted on picturesque, formerly fortified hilltop positions – defence in bygone days against the Mediterranean's once-frequent sea-borne raids.

Istria has long possessed its own culture. Its coastal towns have similarities with those further south. The interior's quite different. In music the Istrians use a scale composed of alternating tones and semitones, found nowhere else in the world. You'll hear tunes and songs using this scale, often rather monotonous sounding, along with music derived from other traditions, in most tourist centres' folklore displays. Some modern composers also use this "Istrian scale" very entertainingly for both "classical" and pop works.

Crossing the border

Let's start from Muggia village on Italian Trieste's southern edge. The minor coast-hugging road takes you across the frontier to **Ankaran**, a tiny spot, with hill-slopes rising immediately inland and a beach backed by trees and grass. The one hotel, built round a former convent, lies at the hamlet's edge. Yugoslav Ankaran's atmosphere strikes you as very similar to Italian Muggia's. In actual fact, thousands of families are split by this frontier. Almost half Trieste's population is Slovenian and Slovenian's the language (see Chapter 19) you'll hear spoken there almost as much as Italian.

Our minor coast road joins Yugoslavia's 1035-km-long M2 "Magistrala" Adriatic highway just before Koper. The M2 links nearly all Yugoslavia's coastal settlements. It's marked M2 on maps, but not yet on all roadsigns.

In Italian Koper's known as Capodistria, "top of Istria". Half industrial city, half international harbour, bustling **Koper** is no longer a major holiday spot, though you can find hotels and other places to stay at if you want them, and a beach to swim from. It's an invigorating mixture of ancient island centre, and up-to-the-minute mainland flats, offices, and factories. A causeway links the two halves.

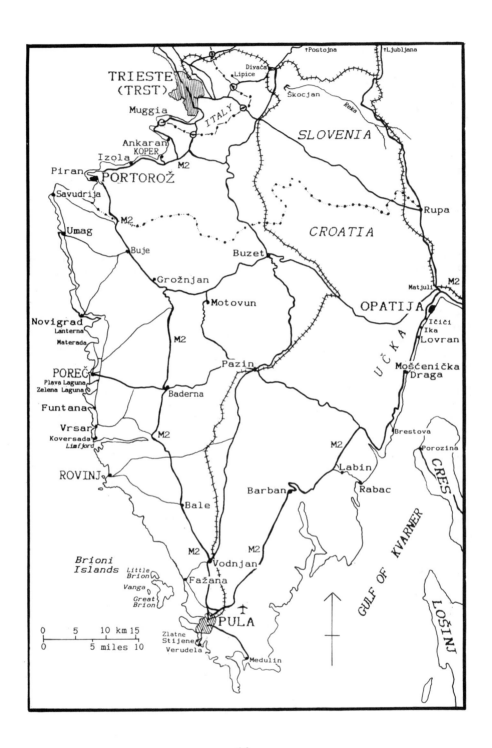

Everyone who arrives by public transport enjoys the wonderful, brightly-painted old railway steam engine standing in the grounds of the busy bus and railway station. There are modern flats and offices within sight.

In contrast, in Titov Trg, (Tito Square), the centre of Koper's island, you're surrounded by a 15th–16th century cathedral with a 13th century belltower beside it, a 13th century Venetian-style "loggia" (a sort of small half-open meeting-place once used for the town elders' councils and for courts hearing lawsuits, built in a style that's regular along this coast which mighty Venice dominated for some 600 years), and a very impressive 13th–14th century Governor's Palace. It's a good introduction to the sort of towns you'll see all along the coast – far more typically Yugoslav than little Ankaran.

Three miles along the M2 the church dominating tiny **Izola** comes into view. As its name implies (it's called Isola in Italian), Izola's another island joined to the mainland by a causeway. It's still a charming little fishing village. You can stay here, too, if you wish, and swim from its pleasant small beach.

Portorož and its surroundings

Piran, the coast's next settlement, lies just off the highway. Here, Tartini Square's bustling quaysides and lively, colourful restaurants and cafés draw crowds of summer visitors. In the middle of the square you'll be struck by a statue of the famous violinist that it's named after. He was born here in 1692. But everything's dominated by a belltower nearly 400 years old and very reminiscent of Venice's famous Campanile. There are actually two towers like this in the town.

Piran's a delightfully quiet spot to stay in. If you explore its tangled alleys you'll soon realise they spread over a small hill peninsula, ringed by remnants of crumbling fortifications. It was once a busy fishing harbour and minor port. Today it's mainly a big, bustling neighbour's quiet suburb, linked by a 10-minute buggy-bus service in high season.

Your first sight of **Portorož** shows a huge, busy, glamorous resort. Modern hotel blocks line the shore and clamber up hillsides immediately inland. They face a broad, curving seaside promenade. It has gardens, with modern shops in the middle of them, and a large man-made, sandy beach, with a little shingle in it, on its further side. It's cleaned every morning.

The first hotel you come to is the Bernardin, a solidly-built sort of modern holiday village. Here you've got your own shops, pleasant small marina, private beach, indoor and outdoor swimming pools, sports facilities, and nightspot. Straightforward, comfortable hotels, like the Slovenija, Riviera, Metropol, Neptun, Grand Palace, and others stretch round the bay, with the modernised old Palace, Portorož's original pre-WWI hotel, and its more recent additions (which include the Grand Palace) towards the further end.

You'll find here lots of open-air restaurants, bars, and shops selling handicrafts, clothes, and food and drink. Several hotels have their own beaches, though the public beach area's also always well patronised. You pay a small fee to use it. Thousands of Yugoslavs, as well as foreign visitors, spend their holidays in Portorož. It has been popular for generations, not least for its thermal baths. There's a major treatment centre just inland from the Grand Palace hotel.

If you enjoy a flutter, you'll find several casinos in Portorož's main hotels. They're open only to foreigners using Western currencies, so take your passport and your traveller's cheques.

If you fancy a long, leisurely meal away from the town's bustle, you'll find restaurants that serve good food just outside the town along the southbound road. Their fish dishes are specially good. The Flambé restaurant in town's good too.

Umag and Novigrad

If you go out of the town past these restaurants you cross after about 12 miles from the Republic of Slovenia into Croatia, another of the country's constituent Republics. There's absolutely nothing to indicate any difference unless you happen to know the two languages (Chapter 19), and read shop window notices and the like.

Savudrija, the first main town on Croatia's enormously long share of coast, lies some 8 miles off the main highway. Today it's just a fishing base. Its only claim to modern fame is the possession of Yugoslavia's most westerly lighthouse.

You reach **Umag** by a five-mile run from Savudrija, or by turning off the main highway at Buje, one of Istria's many once-fortified hilltop towns. Buje was a hill fort even in prehistoric times. Its parish church was built on the remains of a Roman temple.

Your main impression of Umag once you reach your hotel tends to be one of greenery – green trees of many species, masses of flowers, and even coarse grass lawns, all specially planted. After the hilly inland road the ground seems unusually flat. Hotels and apartment villages spread over a pretty large expanse – from the Katoro complex in the south to the Kanegra settlement not far from Savudrija. A small narrow-gauge train links Katoro to the little old town in the middle of all the new developments. Most have their own swimming pools – sometimes more than one – and they're surrounded by long curving beaches and bathing areas. These are mostly rocky, but some are quite wide and spacious.

You can hire boats, bikes, surfboards, and so on, and also use a conveniently-located sports centre for tennis and other games. Strolling quietly under the trees is popular and relaxing. Alternatively, if you're not on the railway side you can take one of the cheap and frequent buses the two or three miles into Umag and explore its tiny streets and medieval squares and quays. The town was knocked about a bit in the war but has a good, brand new shopping centre.

Ten miles south from Umag you come to **Novigrad**, known in full as Novigrad Istra to distinguish it from other Novigrads – the name means Newtown. Here, it's the tennis courts that strike you as you arrive – there seems to be scores of them. The ground's level here, too, which is rare in Yugoslavia. There's plenty of opportunity for watersports, and you can hire bikes and boats.

Novigrad's basically a quiet, relaxing spot. Its long beaches, mostly pebbly, are often shallow and very suitable for children. The level, tree-covered areas immediately inland encourage walking and cycling. The tiny medieval town next to the hotel area occupies a minute flat peninsula. It's dominated by yet another Venetian-style belltower, and you can find traces of old fortifications. Walking or cycling there takes only minutes. Once arrived, you can relax among its alleys or on the quays of the former fishing harbour. Today it's a modern marina full of colourful yachts and motorboats. The short River Mirna reaches the sea in the bay stretching south and east.

Poreč

The resort called **Poreč** is really 9 separate spots (including the actual town) or, if you prefer, a single holiday area scattered over about 12 miles of hilly coast as crows fly, and about twice that far if you count the shore's indentations or the road network's contortions. What has happened is that hotels have been built at almost every suitable spot on the coast inside Poreč commune's boundaries, including the old town itself and an island just a few minutes' boat ride away. Some stand more or less on their own. Others form part of larger and sometimes very highly organised and skilfully laid out holiday complexes.

The most northerly of them takes its name, **Lanterna**, from the wooded headland where it stands. It's the River Mirna estuary's further side from Novigrad. This little tourist settlement, about 8 miles from Poreč town, has been built on a pine-covered, rocky peninsula with a good pebble-and-shingle beach under a steep slope close to the hotels and apartments. If you use Lanterna's sports centre you'll find tennis courts, table tennis, surfboards, water-skiing, motorboats, kayak canoes, rowboats, pedalos and so on can be hired. Children are specially catered for, and there's a

disco and music in the evenings for the grownups.

At **Červar** self-catering apartments have been built round a little marina on one side of a fairly deep bay. The land's pretty broken here, and you've a choice of two rock-and-pebble beaches up to 300 yards away. You can hire surfboards, rowboats, bikes, pedalos, and so on, or play tennis, go water-skiing, or spend time in the bowling alley. There's a supermarket and post office, plenty of places where you can eat out, and live music to dance to on high season evenings. Červar's about 6 miles from Poreč town.

Materada lies a good deal closer – barely 3 miles off. A large hotel here occupies the slopes of another wooded headland, with one pleasant rock-and-pebble beach below it and another one a quarter of an hour's walk away. Here, too, you're well provided with sporting activities, evening entertainment, and restaurants where you can eat out. Children are specially catered for as well.

You'll find a hotel and self-catering apartments at **Spadiči**, in another bay south from Materada and barely 2 miles from the town centre. You've swimming pools as well as a beach here, and a pretty quiet setting.

You mustn't imagine, though, that these resorts north of Poreč are all strung out along a single road. They aren't. You have to keep taking different turnings off a minor road that runs roughly, very roughly, parallel to the coast's general direction. If you try to visit them all you'll drive a maybe 40-mile road trip, much more if you lose your way. Frequent buses going in and out of Poreč do the trip quickly however.

Pical has the same general character as the places just described, but isn't much more than a mile from the main part of Poreč. You've plenty of sporting activities here, including watersports, and a beach only 150 yards away. One of the hotels also possesses its own swimming pool. All this area north of Poreč is reasonably flat, so you can take hired bikes into the old town if you don't want to travel by bus. From Pical area you can also walk. It's part of Poreč's modern section.

As a still-lived-in medieval town **Poreč** proper is extremely attractive. It's built on a tiny peninsula, with a colourful little harbour curled into its southern side. Narrow streets run into and through the town. You can see the remains of fortifying walls at the water's edge on the northern side and charming old houses scattered everywhere.

Poreč's great pride however is a magnificent church, Bishop Euphrasius's Basilica. Its oldest part goes back 1700 years, to the time when Romans were still persecuting Christians and their churches were concealed in private houses. Most of what's obvious today, however, including the superb frescos, dates from before AD 600, with later additions right up to this century. Everything has been superbly restored. The building's in magnificent condition.

Parking when you reach Poreč is hell (try in front of the Robna Kuča department store). Driving round the old town's impossible unless you know it as well as the locals do, and walking makes you hot and sticky. Luckily, wonderful ice creams and pastries seem a Poreč (or maybe Yugoslav?) speciality. The places where you buy them are frequent in the little square at the old town's entrance. The small but spacious-seeming harbour, to your left as you arrive, has more good bars and restaurants overlooking it. The Istarska Konoba (Istrian Inn) some 3 miles inland is specially good.

Of hotels actually in Poreč's old and new town areas some of the most appealing stand right on the colourful quayside. They include the friendly little Parentino (Poreč's Roman name was Parentium), the Riviera, and the Neptun. All have fine views over the sea and St Nicholas Island, facing the harbour. Hotels in the built-up area include the Poreč by the bus station. Others have beaches close by and fairly spacious settings.

As an alternative to staying in the town area, you can find good modern accommodation on St Nicholas Island (**Otok Sveti Nikola**), barely 200 yards off the mainland. It boasts fine views of the old town and frequent motorboat connections. Lots of people feel they enjoy the best of old and up-to-date here. The island's wooded, colourful, and peaceful. Poreč's newer mainland parts, spreading away from the peninsula's neck, are mostly rather straggly.

As you go on south you run into hillier country. You come to **Brulo**, which has a number of hotels and pleasant beaches. It's soon followed by two major tourist settlements – Plava Laguna (Blue Lagoon) and Zelena Laguna (Green Lagoon). Both are built round hilly wooded bays with pebbly beaches, and both have their attractions.

Plava Laguna is the nearer and the smaller, though not as small as some of those to Poreč's north. Its hotels vary in size. Beaches are 200–300 yards from the hotels and are rocky or pebbly. One of the hotels specialises in sports facilities (including even a gymnasium: also bikes, though you'll find the terrain a trifle tough if you go outside the area close to the hotels). Another makes special arrangements for children. Self-catering apartments are plentiful.

At the height of summer **Zelena Laguna**, some 4 miles from Poreč, gives the impression of a rather colourful, busy town, full of abnormally cheerful, mostly lightly clad inhabitants, a lot of whom seem to be carrying tennis rackets. Hotels of varying sizes dominate the rocky, pine-covered slopes round a smallish bay, and facilities of every sort are scattered among them. There's tennis, watersports of every variety, and even a sort of permanent all-the-fun-of-the fair section, with things like shooting ranges and hoop-la. The Zeleni Centar includes a good restaurant and pizza house, as well as lots of shops. There's a large nightclub complex near the Hotel Parentium. Kids and grown-ups of all ages can enjoy themselves at Zelena Laguna.

Both Plava Laguna and Zelena Laguna operate regular launch services to Poreč old town during the high season, in addition to cheap and frequent buses.

On to Rovini

The tiny village of **Funtana**, about 5 miles from Zelena Laguna, has grown into a pleasant small resort. You can walk easily from the village's traditional stone houses, shops, and restaurants to the wooded hotel area above a long rock-and-pebble beach. It's a really peaceful spot, though you're within easy enough reach both of Poreč and of the extremely quiet but attractive fishing village resort of

Vrsar, 4 miles south. The Hotel Funtana caters specially for children. Try the Ideal restaurant on the main road close to it, or the Mirabel near the harbour – though they're not the village's only worthwhile eating places. Funtana may not have made much impact in Britain. But the well-known Yugoslav magazine "Arena" recently gave Funtana its top tourism award.

Vrsar village, neat and tidy, built in the usual traditional stone, stands on one side of a tiny, neat-looking bay. Hotels and self-catering apartments are half-hidden among pines on the opposite side's low hillsides a few hundred yards away. It's difficult to pinpoint any special feature in Vrsar, yet the village and its hotels produce a strong impression of peace and relaxation.

That's very different from **Koversada**. Hardly a mile away, its apartments, tents, touring caravans, restaurants, bars, and shops spread over several acres of yet another of this coast's rocky wooded peninsulas, together with an island covered with scrub and pines close to the coast. Koversada's one of Europe's biggest naturist camps. If you're staying there you're expected to show your resident's card each time you've been outside the camp. But people using the camp have no objection to visitors coming in to look around.

It's a long way from being the only naturist holiday spot on this coast. There are lots of naturist beaches, open to all, that you can relax on close to ordinary resorts. Yugoslavia in fact began encouraging naturism back in the 1960s, and quite a number of Yugoslavs themselves spend summer holidays in places like Koversada. If you're interested, take a careful look at tour operators' brochures.

An extraordinary fjord-like bay with steep, wooded sides, nearly 7 miles deep and never more than 200 or 300 yards wide, cuts into the coast directly south of Koversada. It forces the main road to run through strikingly wooded hill scenery inland of its inner tip. Boat excursions to this **Limfjord** or **Limski Kanal** (Lim Channel) are much appreciated by people holidaying in resorts close to it.

To reach Rovinj you have to turn off the undulating main road either at Brajkovići or at the typically Istrian hilltop town of Bale, and drive either 8 or 10 miles to the coast. The name Brajkovići, incidentally, indicates a village where the original inhabitants all belonged to a family or clan called Brajković. You'll find a lot of place-names like that if you get off the beaten track in Istria.

Rovinj is an outstandingly beautiful former port and fishing village. It's reminiscent in many ways of Venice – the first of many towns we'll see that imitated what it saw in Venice. The church of St Euphemia stands on the peninsula's highest point, with the inevitable Campanile-style belltower beside it. This church however is fairly recent (1763), though you can still see remains of two earlier churches (5th and 9th centuries) on the same site.

An archway marks the original town gate's location. In the little square beyond it you'll find a small four-storey clocktower that's an obvious imitation of the famous Orologio in Venice's St Mark's Square. What's more, as in many places along the coast, you'll see the Lion of St Mark, Venice's sacred emblem, carved on the clocktower's side.

Rovinj's peninsula tip was once an island, as aerial photographs clearly show. But the channel separating it from the mainland was filled in centuries ago when the town began spreading. In the Middle Ages the whole settlement was protected by a double ring of walls. But these too were pulled down and their stones used to build the houses, narrow streets, and tiny squares you see today.

Rovinj has only one hotel in the town (its Captain's Cabin bar's a popular nightspot). Other hotels and apartments are all either at its edges, on pine-covered slopes above long but not very wide beaches, or located on two islands, Katarina Island and Red Island (Crveni Otok). Your mainland accommodation isn't likely to be more than 20 minutes walk from the old town's centre. From the more distant, attractively wooded Red Island it's also 20 minutes by boat. Katarina faces the town from close off the shore.

One of Rovinj's special features is the Monvi entertainments centre, which includes a disco, nightclub, beer cellar, and open-air theatre. The town closes down fairly early however. The last Katarina ferry leaves at midnight. Worthwhile restaurants nearby include the Marina, the Sidro, and the Riva.

Pula

It's a 25-mile run to Pula, with the main road forced a long way inland through woodlands, vineyards, and cultivated farmland by cliffs and craggy inlets. New roads are however being built nearer the sea.

On the way to Pula you may be tempted to make a détour from Vodnjan, yet another of Istria's once-fortified hilltop towns, to **Fažana**. This simple small fishing village has no importance of its own. But it's where you take the ferry to the Brioni Islands or, more accurately, to Great Brion (**Veliki Brion**). This is virtually a place of pilgrimage for Yugoslavs. They come in thousands.

In the postwar years Tito (Chapter 17) had a secluded family home on tiny Vanga Island in the Brioni archipelago. He entertained all sorts of VIP foreign visitors, including Queen Elizabeth II, in a sumptuous house on Veliki Brion. High-level international conferences that helped to shape our modern world were also held at the comfortable Neptun Hotel there.

The **Brioni** (or **Brijuni**) have been declared a National Park. Access is restricted to a tiny area close to your landing-place on Great Brion. In a way this is a pity. The islands contain a lot that's of tremendous interest. Apart from extensive Roman and Byzantine remains and important relics of recent history, Great Brion possesses vast park-like green landscapes more reminiscent of southern Britain than of the warm Mediterranean. Before World War II it was a very select, carefully tended holiday spot. When Tito made it his own he indulged his passion for wildlife and nature conservation and filled Great Brion with even more plants and trees and animals, including a small safari park. It's magnificent today. You can holiday at the comfortable Neptun and nearby Istra hotels. Tennis and horseriding are available.

The islands' environment's very fragile. The distance you and the thousands of day visitors who cross from Fažana are allowed to travel is limited to an area close to the hotels and to a narrow-gauge train trip in the vicinity. Millions of Yugoslavs and even more millions worldwide would dearly love to explore not only Great Brion but also tiny Vanga, where Tito

had his family hideaway for so many years. But they have to be disappointed. Vanga's so small it would quickly disappear if all interested visitors were allowed to land. Great Brion's greenness would vanish very fast too.

Pula lies under 10 miles from the Brioni. Reading the brochures makes you think Pula's a very popular resort indeed. So it had better be made clear that Pula town is completely separate from the three major resorts 3 to 8 miles from it (but still in Pula commune). The only hotel in the town itself is the large, long-established Riviera, close to the harbour and the Roman amphitheatre.

Zlatne Stijene (Golden Rocks), about 2 miles southeast of the town centre, is the nearest holiday spot. Golden Rocks is a pretty apt description. The resort's built on the tip of a rock-ringed peninsula, with hotels and apartments rising in tiers among shady pines that seem to grow much of the time direct from bare rock. There's enough flat ground for tennis courts. You have to be normally fit, though, to cope with the steps going up and down from the beach and maybe also from the hotel restaurant and swimming pool. If you've spare energy you can use the extensive sports centre at neighbouring Verudela. Apart from organised sightseeing excursions, buses go regularly to Pula.

Although **Verudela** lies so close, you're totally unaware of Zlatne Stijene's existence on a neighbouring headland while you're in Verudela. It has a number of hotels of varying types beautifully tucked away in shaded pinewoods on the top of its high, rocky peninsula. They're all reasonably close to the sports centre which offers scores of tennis courts and a lot of other activities and entertainments. There's even a hall large enough to accommodate mass chess tournaments.

You enjoy lots of attractive seaward views through the pines on the high, rocky peninsula's top. Swimming in the open sea however involves a bit of a climb down to the beach and back again. Some hotels have swimming pools.

The **Ribarska Koliba** (Fisherman's Cottage) apartments and other self-catering accommodation are also located on this peninsula, mostly on slightly lower ground, often with steps down to the beach. The whole region's served by quite frequent buses to Pula.

The third main resort, **Medulin**, lies about 8 miles southeast of Pula town. It's close to a tiny old fishing village on a headland just east of Istria's southernmost tip. Like Verudela, Medulin offers a sports centre and a choice of hotels, one of which makes special arrangements for children.

Because the bay it stands on is well-sheltered you can enjoy a full range of watersports here, from windsurfing to pedalos. And you don't have to exert yourself climbing down to the beach or back again. The ground's pretty flat. Buses go into Pula at fixed times.

As for **Pula** itself, you'll almost certainly find this extraordinary town rather unattractive at first sight. Ugly shipyards and dusty factories are its most obvious features, with an enormous Roman amphitheatre soaring up on slightly higher land close to them, with a small park directly below it. However, if you've any taste for old places you'll find that the more you explore Pula the more you'll find to enjoy.

Its earliest inhabitants left their traces 40,000 years ago, and you can see a few bits of 8000-year-old "Cyclopean" masonry – stone blocks weighing many tons each, which prehistoric peoples built their fortresses with in many Mediterranean spots. The Romans left the famous amphitheatres, well worth a visit. It's almost 2000 years old and used today for events like Pula's well-known July film festival.

They also left remains of their little port and two small temples, both still virtually complete and of roughly the same data as the amphitheatre. One's dedicated to the Emperor Augustus, and the other to the huntress goddess Diana. 700 years ago Pula's town hall was built onto the back of the second temple. To make everything more confusing, you'll find a 6th century Byzantine Orthodox church on the opposite side of the Roman town centre, one of several built while the Byzantine emperors controlled the town. And these are only a few of Pula's ancient remains. Two of the Roman town's gates are still standing, for instance. If you're interested you should also visit the town's Archaeological Museum of Istria.

You need a good street map to explore Pula properly. You can buy them in stationers. Some coach tours however manage to give you a good idea of the town. Car-and-passenger ferries link Pula with Rimini in Italy and with Mali Lošinj and Zadar (Chapters 5 and 6).

Istria's other coast

Though we're still on the M2 Magistrala, the "Adriatic Highway", most of which was built only in the 1960s, we're set now to change course up Istria's eastern side. Because of high hills sloping down to the sea and endless coastal indentations the main road's forced to keep several miles inland, with only very occasional turnings down to the sea. We come first to hilltop **Barban**, with a lot of attractive old houses and a hairpin descent on its further side, and then to medieval **Labin**, similarly perched on its hill, though with extensive later modern additions.

Here we can turn off for the 4-mile run down to **Rabac**. This is an almost wholly modern resort, set in a crescent bay ringed by steep hillsides covered with Mediterranean pines and red-roofed modern homes, many of which offer rooms for visitors. Rabac has a large, wide pebbly beach, backed by a stretch of coarse grass and trees. A few minutes away, round the bay, you come to the original tiny fishing harbour and village. There are restaurants, bars, and shops catering for visitors here today. The whole bay's very sheltered.

Not all hotels are at beach level. Some perch on the hillsides. One or two provide swimming pools and also tennis courts and space for other games. Many visitors revel in Rabac's seclusion. It has become very popular with British visitors.

Back on the main road on the eastern side of Labin's old town centre, we finally turn toward the sea about 20 miles further on and begin a long run on a high corniche road that descends very slowly and ends only as we're approaching Opatija, Istria's second sophisticated, long-established, large resort.

The views along the coast from most of this road are superb. Before you've gone far you see a well-signposted steep turning down to the ferry at **Brestova**, which takes you on the short crossing to Porozina if you're bound for Cres or Mali Lošinj (Chapter 5).

A few miles on you pass first little Brseč village and then inland Mošćenice, high on the mountainside. By now you're descending towards **Mošćenička Draga** (Mošćenice Bay), a pleasant, quiet small spot, squeezed between 5000-foot Mount Učka's lower slopes, covered with pines, laurels, wild cherries and other trees, and the sea. It boasts two modern hotels, one fairly large. But building space is limited, and modern bustle isn't really possible.

Another two or three miles take you to **Medveja**, a little bigger than Mošćenička Draga, but still squeezed between Mount Učka and the sea, with its streets usually a tangle of traffic. It has a modern hotel and a few modern self-catering apartments. The rocky beach is quite pleasant, and so are the town's bars and restaurants.

It's another short run to **Lovran**, much bigger than either of its southern neighbours. You'll find Lovran a pleasant mixture of modern and older buildings – and that applies to its hotels as well. The Excelsior's a large, extremely well-appointed modern hotel, with sun terraces dropping down to the sea, and floodlit tennis courts, a bowling alley, and high season nightclub. Other smaller establishments are rather elegant, well-modernised pre-war buildings, maybe standing in their own wooded grounds. Despite all the traffic, Lovran will strike you as basically peaceful and relaxed. The beach is rocky. If you like walking, some good, steep inland rambles are possible.

Opatija

Ika and **Ičiči** each provides its own

accommodation and its own beach. But they're really outlying suburbs of large, sophisticated, crowded, and always busy Opatija.

Opatija strikes everyone as having a character all its own. Though not quite as constricted by Mount Učka as smaller places to the south, it still seems to consist mainly of one, long very crowded and very busy main street, which twists and turns, and finally disappears southward to Ičiči over an appreciably steep hill. This impression's a bit false. Opatija stretches inland – often uphill – more than is obvious at first sight, and one or two of its inland hotels are very pleasantly located.

Most people however want to be close to the sea, and more and more hotels have been packed in along the main road. The oldest, the Kvarner and its sister, the Villa Amalia, still maintain the lovely spacious gardens that were so much appreciated between the wars and even before World War I. But they're the exceptions. Only a few much more modest inland establishments have competing garden settings. And they're some way from the shore.

Some hotels have private beaches and some have swimming pools. Some provide free admission to Opatija's huge, mostly rocky public bathing area. All Opatija's beach areas tend to become pretty crowded in July and August, as do all its bars and shops and restaurants and discos and everything else. But that's part of the place's appeal.

High season life goes on well into the night, and runs to opera and classical concerts as well as discos and nightclubs. You don't go to Opatija for peace and quiet, not in summer, at least. If you want to be within reach of all the bustle, and at the same time enjoy a feeling of slightly greater space, try the Ambassador Hotel on the town's northern edge in what used to be the separate Volosko hamlet. For a little temporary peace you can stroll along very pleasant coastal paths going all the way to Lovran in one direction and to Volosko in the other. Hotels right on the seafront, like the Kvarner and the Villa Amalia have gates into their gardens from this path.

The town's name, incidentally, means Abbey – a reference to the tiny abbey whose ruins you can still see in the elegant town centre park near the Kvarner Hotel. In Austro-Hungarian days and between the wars the name's Italian version, Abbazia, was used, and that's how the town's referred to in many older guidebooks.

Access

Resorts on Istria's west coast are reached mainly via Pula airport, though Ljubljana (Chapter 10) may be used for the more northerly, Krk-Rijeka airport (Chapter 5) is closest for Opatija and resorts near it. Transfer times rarely exceed 1½ hours.

Excursions

Excursions vary a little in this region. One from Istria's western side that's extremely popular and well worthwhile takes you on a full-day outing to **Venice**. That unique town needs a whole book to itself. But a day there gives you a chance to enjoy its extraordinary beauty (even though much is pretty tumbledown today), and to see some of its great sights. You can proably fit in St Mark's Square, St Mark's basilica, the Doge's Palace, the Bridge of Sighs leading from the palace to the prison, the

Grand Canal, the Rialto Bridge, and some of the town's remarkable churches and little squares, to say nothing of its innumerable bridges.

If you bear in mind that for a thousand years Venice was one of Europe's most powerful states, and that for 600 of those years it controlled virtually all the towns on Yugoslavia's coast, you'll begin to understand why so many of the towns imitated Venice in building styles and almost everything else. In exchange, Venice recruited thousands of her seamen from the Yugoslav coast. The name Riva degli Schiavoni, given to the vital quayside just beyond the Doge's Palace, makes that clear.

Full-day coach trips from all Istria's resorts take you to the enormous **Postojna Caves**, a chain of magnificent limestone caverns that's among the world's largest. You cover the first 1½ miles on a little train, with a lot of walking still to come. You see a tremendous variety of stalactites and stalagmites and superb cave scenery. Postojna's located about 27 miles northeast of Trieste. Routes from the resorts vary. All give you a good view of Istria's countryside.

If you're interested in the limestone scenery of this Kras region (which gave the term "karst" to the world's geographers: it's most obvious characteristic is a relative absence of surface water such as rivers) you may like to make for the Škocjan Caves (Škocjanske jame) near Divača on the road from the northern Istrian resorts to Postojna. They have one of the world's biggest underground rivers running through them in a 450-foot-high subterranean canyon, but have only recently been organised for tourists. In 1986 they were added to UNESCO's world heritage list.

Long all-day coach outings take you to

Ljubljana, the Slovenian Republic's beautiful capital, and to the long-famous summer-and-winter mountain resort of **Bled**. Both are described in Chapter 10.

A popular shorter excursion from the more northerly resorts on Istria's western side takes you to **Motovun**. We've mentioned several of Istria's formerly-fortified hilltop towns, but haven't shown you much in the way of fortifications. Motovun has managed to preserve a lot of its medieval appearance. You enter by a truly magnificent set of gateway fortifications, and can explore ancient streets and buildings. Views from the top are superb on clear days.

From these same resorts it's also possible to explore **Trieste**, just across the Italian border. There's plenty to interest visitors here. But its main appeal is its magnificent setting – a huge amphitheatre of hills sweeping down to a long curving stretch of coast. On the way you get plentiful views of changing countrysides.

Lipice (or Lipica), the stables and stud farm where the white Lipizzaner horses that were the Austrian Emperors' pride and joy originated, attract thousands of visitors every year. If you've any interest at all in horses and horsemanship you'll enjoy Lipice. If you're skilled enough and have your jodhpurs and riding boots with you, you'll even be allowed to ride the horses yourself.

Motorboat trips to the **Limfjord** have already been mentioned. They're among many shorter sea trips you can make from one resort to another, or from your hotel to an old town close to it. Boat excursions which end with a picnic meal of freshly-cooked seafood are also popular.

For **Rab** and **Plitvice National Park** see Chapter 5.

Chapter Five

The Gulf of Kvarner

Strictly speaking, Istria's eastern side, which we looked at in our last chapter, forms the Gulf of Kvarner's western boundary. But it's easier to treat that as part of Istria and to describe in this chapter the so-called "Kvarner islands", together with the "Croatian littoral" and its extension down the Gulf's eastern flank.

On this side of the Gulf the coast changes considerably. For the first 45 miles it consists in effect of the Kapela Mountains' foothills. Most of the range's peaks lie under 15 miles from the sea. But they rise to over 5000 feet, and for a good six months of the year you've snow here capable of providing excellent skiing. In fact, a brand new ski resort now being built on Mount Bjelolasica, the Kapela's highest point, put in a bid for the 1992 Winter Olympics back in 1986.

At Senj, where our first 45 miles ends, the scenery becomes dramatic. For the next 80 miles the Velebit's violently gaunt, bare mountain ridge rising sheer from the sea dominates everything. Its highest point tops Bjelolasica by 800 feet but it's barely 7 miles from the sea.

A tangled scattering of islands fills the Gulf. Those in the north are mainly covered with woods. In the south they become increasingly bare and white, like lunar landscapes. Their vegetation has been destroyed partly by grazing goats, and partly by winds sweeping down from the Velebit. The only greenery you see on them lies in little wind-sheltered hollows.

The coast's temperatures are baking in summer but stay mild in winter. In October you can be sunbathing beside the sea but find yourself standing in 18 inches of early snow when you cross the Velebit to the Lika valley behind it. Between Rijeka and the ridge's southern end, 120 miles away, only two surfaced roads cross passes leading inland.

Rijeka

Rijeka, 6 hilly miles from Opatija, occupies the Gulf of Kvarner's northernmost point. It's a busy port, industrial town, and shipbuilding centre today. Its history goes back to prehistoric times. The old town centre's still laid out largely as the Romans left it. Yet you're unlikely to be much attracted by Rijeka. Almost the only holidaymakers it interests are people travelling on their own. For them it's a major communications centre. Long-distance buses take you from here to the southernmost part of the coast and to many inland towns. Trains link with the lines serving all Yugoslavia's major inland areas.

You'll find bus and rail stations close together on the main Opatija road. A few minutes beyond them you come to the quays where comfortable car-and-passenger ferries carry you and your car to Venice in one direction and to Greece (Corfu and Igoumenitsa) in the other. They make intermediate stops at main points on Yugoslavia's coast. These include Zadar, Split, Dubrovnik, and Bar, all described in later chapters. Slower ferries make more stops and don't go beyond Yugoslav ports. They're a fascinating way to see the coast. Everyone should make at least one sea journey along the coast. The views are unforgettable. Until the Magistrala Adriatic Highway was completed in the 1960s you had to travel up and down the coast by boat unless you wanted to smash your car's suspension to bits on the cart track cut in virgin rock by Napoleon's Marshal Marmont. If you keep your eyes open while you're driving on the Magistrala you can still see occasional remnants of Marmont's unbearably bumpy track.

The "Croatian Littoral"

The name's hardly ever used today. But it's a useful title for the little string of resorts at the northern end of the Gulf of Kvarner's eastern side. They became well known a hundred years ago when the railway reached close enough to make them accessible to well-off folk from the capital of what was then the Austro-Hungarian province of Croatia, Zagreb. Wealthy people going on holiday (then a fairly novel idea) from the Austro-Hungarian Empire's capital, Vienna, and from other parts of Austria took the new-fangled train for preference to Opatija or Portorož or Venice.

You're hardly clear of Rijeka's suburbs before you see, just off the road, the little tunny-fishing harbour of **Bakar**. The things that look telegraph poles set at 75° to vertical hold strong nets that the fish are driven into.

Bakar's not a holiday resort. But **Bakarac**, at the other end of the bay you're looking into, boasts a couple of small motels, much used by passing motorists. We're on the main southbound part of the M2 Adriatic Highway now. Cars and coaches heading south come from Trieste via the Škofje frontier crossing and drive to Rijeka via the hill town of Buzet and Matulji village, once well-known as the rail terminus for Opatija. This road has recently been much improved. If they've by-passed Trieste on the Italian motorway their crossing-point is Kozina and they reach Rijeka through Rupa. But from Bakar on there's only a single road to the southern coast's increasingly popular holiday spots.

It has been constantly widened and improved at many points since it was built in the 1960s. But you'll see for yourself that further widening is virtually impossible on the stretches which cling precariously to the Velebit's steep slopes. A grandiose-sounding plan has been mooted to link the Kvarner islands nearest the coast with bridges and build a motorway across them to link with the Magistrala on flatter ground near Zadar.

A tiny step in this direction has been taken with the bridge now linking Kraljevica, just beyond Bakarac, with Krk island (for pronunciation see Chapter 19). Krk–Rijeka international airport serves this region, and the bridge makes access easy and fast. Expensive though the offshore motorway would be it would cost less, and cause less disruption, than trying to improve the existing road.

Kraljevica itself has a smallish, mainly rocky beach and a sizeable tourist settlement just south of the town where you can stay.

Ten miles beyond it we reach

Crikvenica, queen of the region's resorts. One of its main attractions is its vast beach of sand and fine shingle, a good mile long. Another is the area's lush vegetation, the result of a very favourable climate. On the hillsides it's mainly pines and cypresses that you see, with palms and many other tree varieties in town. But Crikvenica has magnificent, flower-filled parks as well.

The Therapia Hotel, built in the days of Austro-Hungarian splendour and named when sea-bathing was the in thing for health (therapia is the Greek word that we use as "therapy"), still dominates the town. The gardens round it are lovely. Though totally modernised, with indoor and outdoor seawater swimming pools, tennis courts and so on, it's still old world-elegant. The gardens slope down to a fairly narrow section of public beach.

Other more modest establishments have also been excellently modernised and a number of new ones built, the latest in 1985. They haven't however overwhelmed the town's well-mellowed atmosphere. In the high season Crikvenica's now again a very lively spot, and seems to have music everywhere. It's built on a long ribbon of land, and because the Magistrala has been re-routed along an inland bypass traffic isn't a major problem.

Selce is to some extent a suburb of Crikvenica, but a resort in its own right at the same time. It lies a bit off the main road in a pleasantly sheltered bay. It's altogether smaller and more modest than its large neighbour, but has a very similar beach. You'll find the usual range of bars and entertainment here. And the town's equally well placed for excursions (see end of chapter).

Novi Vinodolski, the last of these "Croatian Littoral" resorts, lies 4 miles beyond Selce. Like its nearest neighbour it possesses several sizeable hotels, including two with facilities like swimming pools and saunas, but offers far more accommodation in private rooms. The town has a fine-shingle beach. Apart from Magistrala traffic it's basically a quiet, modest place. Its main claim to fame is that its castle, once a stronghold of the powerful medieval Frankopan family, was where Croatia's first code of laws, the Vinodol Code, was promulgated (Vinodol's the region's name).

While Novi's the last of this string of resorts you'll find occasional small places where you can stay overnight if you're driving down the coast – or longer, of course, if you like the spot.

The Velebit road

The next 100 miles of coast are among the most spectacular. They start with a fairly uneventful run of 20-odd miles to Senj. You pass a few small villages. The largest is **Klenovica**, which boasts a quite comfortable tiny hotel. But from Senj on the scenery becomes extraordinary. The road you're on is just a ribbon precariously notched into the Velebit's long, bare, steep western side, with the summits out of sight thousands of feet above you. Most of the settlements – they're not exactly numerous – lie a long way down at the water's edge, reached by tiny, steep roads.

Senj itself is different. It's a medium-sized, attractive little town actually on the M2 highway at the foot of the first of the Velebit's two motorable, surfaced-road crossings. If you go a little way up the winding road leading to the 2000-foot Vratnik saddle between the Velebit's northern end and the Kapela range you'll get a fine

view over Senj, the coast, and Krk and smaller offshore islands. If you want to take photographs do remember that it's strictly forbidden to stop even for a moment on the roadway itself (see Chapter 18). Ferries link Senj with Lopar on Rab island.

Senj offers restaurants, an open-air market, a small modern hotel, and nearly 1000 rooms in private houses. It's an excellent overnight stopping-place, and attractive to wander round. The buildings are nearly all of traditional stone. Its ruined castle, built by the powerful Frankopan family around 1300, once sheltered much-feared Uskoks (Uskoci) – inland Croat and Serb refugees from Turks invading overland, who continued their war against the Turks at sea with such ferocity that it was widely believed they ate the hearts of enemies they killed. The fort high above the town, still virtually intact, was built by the Turks in 1558. It's called Nehaj – Dreadnought. Part of the town's walls can still be seen. A lot more was standing till destroyed in World War II battles.

For the 80-odd miles beyond Senj the road becomes distinctly lonely. **Jurjevo**, 6 miles from Senj, stands actually on the road, with its older buildings all constructed of traditional stone. Its restaurants offer a useful lunch-stop. There's also a medium-sized modern hotel, a pansion (Chapter 18), and hundreds of private rooms. Jurjevo was once fortified. You can still see remains of its walls on its seaward side. Roman remains are pretty thick on the ground around here too.

Beyond Jurjevo the road clings higher to the Velebit's slope, and such villages as exist lie mostly far below, right at the water's edge. They include colourful little Starigrad (Old Town), called Starigrad pod Velebit (Starigrad under Velebit) or **Starigrad Podgorje** (Starigrad Underhill) to distinguish it from other Starigrads we'll be meeting.

From near Starigrad you become very aware of Rab Island lying close to the coast. From **Jablanac**, 40 miles from Senj and reached by steep roads down from the Magistrala, you can take a ferry to Mišnjak on Rab, or to Stara Novalja on Pag (Chapter 6), or make a circular trip linking all three spots. Jablanac becomes crowded in summer. It has tiny hotels and places to swim from.

On this stretch of coast the road has been pushed continuously further up the mountain's steep side. Its highest point is actually 1300 feet above the sea. And there's no settlement of any size till you reach Karlobag, some 16 miles away. Driving at night gets lonely.

Karlobag is important because it lies at the foot of the road up to the 3000-foot Oštarije Pass over the Velebit. The hairpin bends immediately above Karlobag provide superb views of the coast, bare, white Pag island, and the Velebit's forbidding slopes that become colourful in spring with all sorts of wild flowers and fragrant with herbs like sage, thyme, and rosemary. The ferry from Karlobag to Pag town cuts distances to some Pag destinations for southbound travellers.

The 40 miles from Karlobag to Maslenica at the Velebit's southern end are about the loneliest of all on this coastal section. The only village of any note is **Starigrad Paklenica**. It takes the distinctive part of its name from the small Paklenica National Park, high above it on the Velebit. The park includes spectacular scenery, including a canyon 1000 feet deep and

a smaller one that's even wilder. There's a sizeable hotel here, and a pleasant small resort on a fairly wide shelf of land at the Velebit's foot. The beach is rocky. The open area surrounding the hotel is partly tree-covered and attractive.

The sports you can enjoy here include tennis, bowling, volleyball, and canoeing, as well as watersports in the well-sheltered waters between Pag and the mainland. And despite its seeming isolation Starigrad Paklenica's very well placed for excursions in all directions – to Zadar, to the Plitvice National Park, to Pag and other islands, and further afield as well. Excursions are outlined below.

Cres and Lošini

At Starigrad Paklenica we've already reached Dalmatia proper's northern boundary. We must return to the Gulf of Kvarner's north to look at the Gulf's numerous islands, four of which have for years been attracting more and more holidaymakers.

We start with Cres and Lošinj. If that makes them sound like inseparable twins – well, in a way they are. They're the crest of a 50-mile-long submerged mountain ridge. They're joined today by a bridge, and in places both become extremely narrow. Stretches of dark green Mediterranean pine cover much of their land. Olives are plentiful too. Despite a good deal of modern building villages are still small and infrequent. The two islands have an appealing atmosphere of being well away from the world's bustle. And they're reached quickly from Pula airport via the Brestova–Porozina ferry (Chapter 4).

One of Cres island's oddities is its freshwater Lake Vrana. The lake's floor is 225 feet below sea level.

The main resorts lie on the outskirts of the island's two capitals, the towns of **Cres** and **Mali Lošinj**. Cres lies towards its island's north and Mali Lošinj (Little Lošinj) in its island's southerly part. A Veli Lošinj (Big Lošinj) exists only a mile or two from the "Little" town. But it's actually smaller than its "little" neighbour.

Mali Lošinj is the bigger resort of the two. You'll be one of up to 1200 guests here, accommodated in two hotels. Both have their own beaches, and the smaller has a swimming pool and sports centre as well. You won't find the entertainment riotous. But there's a feeling of tremendous spaciousness, of sea and sky in every direction. In addition to being able to enjoy many of the excursions described in Chapter 4 you'll find that trips to neighbouring small islands are also available.

The towns of Cres and Mali Lošinj both have a lot that appeals to visitors. Cres was once important enough to have been walled. It has a town gate with a clock in it, a typically Venetian belltower, the former Governor's palace, an arsenal, a granary where grain was stored for emergency use, and a few elegant patrician mansions in Venetian style. Mali Lošinj possesses another Venetian belltower. In Veli Lošinj the most striking feature is a solid Venetian tower erected 400 years ago for protection against marauding Uskoks.

All three little towns have quaysides where everyone likes to stand and stare. The well-weathered stone architecture of even the most modest houses is pure joy. Though the islands are only a few hundred yards wide in places, their hills rise to between 600 and 2000 feet.

The island of Krk

Unlike nearly all Yugoslavia's other offshore islands Krk isn't long and narrow. It's actually made up of the submerged crest-ridges of some three mountain ranges, with valleys between. Much of the land's relatively flat, and much is covered with woods. The highest point, between Punat and Baška in the south, rises to some 1800 feet. The airport, well under an hour by road from Rijeka, is located in the island's north.

The town of **Krk** (Grad Krk to distinguish it from Otok Krk) is the island's capital and also its main resort, with a number of hotels of varying sizes, all run by the same concern, spread round the town's sheltered south-facing bay. Like Cres and Mali Lošinj you'll find it a decidedly Venetian-looking town, and one that appeals strongly to its regular visitors. Many return year after year. Though the resort area's fairly large, it has the air of slight remoteness common to so many island locations. Centuries ago, Krk was a town of considerable importance. You feel it's enjoying well-earned retirement now.

Punat, a few miles to Krk's east, occupies one side of the narrow entrance to an almost landlocked bay – ideal watersports territory. Your hotels form part of a small resort area just outside the village. The beach is rocky. Apart from the stone-built houses typical of the whole coast's fishing villages, you'll see here a few 18th century homes with the outside stone staircases then normal.

Still further south, **Baška**, another typical fishing village, has become another much-appreciated resort, with modern hotels on the village's edge.

Malinska, Njivice, and Omišalj are

stretched out along Krk's northwest coast. The tiny village of **Malinska** has a large holiday complex stretching along the rocky shore close to it. Extensive and very colourful gardens surround a big hotel, large numbers of terraced self-catering apartments, and beach bars and the like. The whole complex is set against thousands of Mediterranean pines.

Njivice, barely 2 miles from Malinska, is similarly based on a tiny fishing harbour and village in another bay ringed by pines. You'll notice that the Hotel Jadran here, though modern and white and not built of traditional stone, contrives to give a very good imitation of traditional-style architecture, especially in its buildings beside the tiny harbour. The long beach is rocky, with cemented sunbathing areas. You can play tennis here, and hire surfboards, rowboats, motorboats, and bicycles. The terrain in and round the resort's pretty flat.

The third of these holiday spots, **Omišalj**, is also spread out along a long, rocky shore, with lots of bays and inlets. It has its own tiny harbour and quayside buildings. The town's main part however was originally based on one of the island's five Frankopan hilltop settlements. Its citadel-fortress has disappeared. But you can still follow the tangled medieval street layout of the town that grew up around it. You can walk up to it along paths winding through pines, cypresses, and olive trees.

Rab Island

South of Krk, Rab island's main characteristic always appears to be its colourfulness. It's a very green island, whose hills you hardly notice though the highest point rises over 1200 feet. The tree species vary considerably,

with plane, sorbus, cherry, fig and cypress as well as Mediterranean pine and various sub-tropical flowering species. And gleaming through them all are the houses' red-tiled roofs.

Rab town is outstandingly colourful. It occupies a narrow peninsula facing a very deep, narrow bay on one side and open sea on the other. On the open side the town walls look down on low cliffs and rocks. They're topped by four very distinctive church belltowers, and there's a delightful cemented path along the rocks below them. You can swim from here. The very sheltered harbour faces into the bay. In the town itself, between harbour and seaward walls, you'll find a tangle of medieval alleys and little squares. The stone they're paved with has the glow produced by centuries of passing pedestrians' feet. Steps lead down beyond the walls to the rock promenade and beach on its further side. Historians tell us that Rab's population today is only a fifth of what it was 500 years ago.

Some of the town's hotels are located on its harbour front, some a little beyond the quayside at the harbour's innermost point, some on the harbour's further side (surrounded by a fine garden area), and some in a bay about 4 miles west. If you stay in the town itself you can enjoy the comings and goings of people and boats along the waterfront and relax in cafés and bars. But you've an appreciable walk to a rocky beach. The other hotels have smallish rocky/pebbly beaches near them. All the hotels have tennis courts and swimming pools, and you can hire surfboards and kayak-canoes. In high season there's a good service of buses and boats in and out of town and to nearby beaches.

There's no problem about the beach

at **Lopar**, 8 miles away in the island's north. It's vast – over a mile long – and sandy, and right outside your hotel. And it shelves very gently, so that it's an ideal spot to take your children – particularly since traffic is extremely light. The youngsters also have their own swings on the beach. You can hire canoes and tennis courts. Buses take you into Rab town.

At **Supetarska Draga**, on a sheltered bay in the island's north but reached by a different road from Lopar, you've another quiet resort. It consists mainly of self-catering apartments facing onto a shingly beach. Like the whole of the island its background is woods.

Access and excursions

You reach Cres and Lošinj from Pula airport via the Brestova–Porozina ferry. Krk and Rab are served by Rijeka–Krk airport and the ferry to Lopar on Rab. Motorists can also use the Kraljevica–Vos, and Crikvenica–Šilo ferries for Krk, and the Senj–Lopar route for Rab (but see also Chapter 18).

Excursions

From the Croatian Littoral resorts – Crikvenica and the others – you can make many of the same excursions as those available in and from Istria. Day trips to Opatija are popular from resorts on Cres, Lošinj, and Rab, and also from Crikvenica and neighbouring spots. There are many local excursions too – from Krk to Rab and vice versa, to tiny islands close to Krk, Rab, Cres, and Lošinj.

The loveliest outing however is to the **Plitvice National Park** lying on hilly ground beyond the towering Velebit.

You'll find the journey there and back over the Velebit, into the fertile, heavily cultivated Lika valley, and on over more thickly-wooded hills to Plitvice well repays the effort of an early rise, should that be necessary.

Plitvice's listed by UNESCO as an outstanding natural heritage of worldwide importance. It's an extraordinary spot, where you can see Yugoslavia's strange karst scenery in the process of formation. The Postojna and Škocjan and other caves in what's known as Yugoslavia's "western karst" area represent more advanced stages. At Plitvice sixteen main lakes at varying heights, many interlinked by waterfalls, are fed by streams rising high on mountain slopes. The whole area's magnificently wooded, with masses of wild flowers, many of them very rare. Wildlife includes bears and a host of other animals.

Letting everyone wander at will over this wild area's many square miles did so much damage that it was decided to limit ordinary visitors to fixed paths, many made of duckboards so that the damp soil isn't worn away. The scheme has worked extremely well. You walk miles at Plitvice without even retracing your steps. You see everything there is to be seen without damaging a thing. And there are very comfortable hotels, good restaurants and cafés, boats for hire, and trips to be made on the largest of the lakes. A little train shows you the main sightseeing points without effort on your part. Kayaking's possible on the lower Korana, the river that feeds most of Plitvice's lakes. The scenery's very striking. Packages direct to Plitvice are available from UK.

Chapter Six

Northern Dalmatia

At Starigrad Paklenica (see Chapter 5) we crossed into ancient Dalmatia province. Here you'll find all the main towns, and many minor ones too, built in wonderful luminous grey-white stone. Their main buildings and their layouts go back centuries – in some cases over 1000 years. Streets and squares paved with the same white stone glow in the most amazing way, thanks to the polishing they've received from millions of feet over hundreds of years. The towns' architecture has had the admiration of architects for centuries.

The Venetians bought Dalmatia province from the Hungarian King for 100,000 ducats in 1420, after a Tatar invasion had weakened his power by penetrating as far as Trogir (Chapter 7). The Venetians had already fought 21 campaigns in the previous 200 years trying to wrest Dalmatia from Hungarian control.

That may all seem a long time ago now and possibly irrelevant. Yet it decided the appearance of the remarkable towns you see today. Whether they and their inhabitants came wholly under Venetian control, as most did, or whether they remained independent or semi-independent, like Dubrovnik and Kotor (Chapters 9 and 10), Venice was everyone's model. When communications depended on sailing boats or oared galleys at sea and, at best, on mules on land, most sizeable towns existed as virtually separate states. And each looked up to Venice, admired Venice and everything Venetian, and aped Venetian architecture and Venetian ways of government.

Many contributed a war galley, or more than one, to Venice's fleet. And Venice's seapower, supreme in the Mediterranean for 1000 years, depended far more than is usually realised on the captains and crews she recruited along the coast of what's now Yugoslavia.

On land however, the Turks had the whip hand. In 1635 a formal treaty between them and Venice fixed the frontier from Starigrad Podgorje (Chapter 5) to Budva (Chapter 9) as the crest of the mountains nearest the sea. The result was that for centuries the Dalmatians lived with the Venetians dominating their waterfront and the Turks entrenched maybe 2 or 3 miles away and few places more than 15 or 20. Not surprisingly, hospitable though they are to friends, you'll find them extremely tough in other ways. They've spent centuries fighting for their freedom.

The road to Zadar – via Nin

Just before little **Maslenica** village at the foot of the Velebit's southern end, a road forks left from the Magistrala to the mining town of Obrovac. It circles north and up the Lika valley to Gospić and the Plitvice National Park

(Chapter 5). The Magistrala itself turns southwest and begins what seems a long downhill run to the lovely town of Zadar.

Your first major landmark's the magnificent high Maslenica Bridge, crossing a narrow channel leading to the landlocked bay known as the Novigradsko More (Novigrad Sea). The bridge has to be so high because the narrow channel's an international seaway leading not only to the Novigradsko More but also up the River Zrmanja's picturesque gorge to Obrovac's bauxite-loading quays.

Novigrad itself is one of the loveliest spots in Dalmatia. From high on the rocky hills to its south you look across the village, its dark red roofs, and its tiny, very well-sheltered harbour to the vast Velebit range beyond. You can reach Novigrad by a road turning left from the little village of Posedarje, two or three miles beyond the Maslenica Bridge. It's distinguished from other Novigrads by the name Novigrad pri Zadar (Novigrad near Zadar). You'll find a small hotel and plenty of private room accommodation here.

Just short of Posedarje a turning on your right takes you to long, thin Pag Island, which you looked onto on your right all the way from Jablanac below the Velebit (see Chapter 5). You cross to the island by another fine iron bridge. For much of the way you've the sea on both sides of you, and only occasional patches of vegetation. It's a very striking run.

You reach **Pag** town about 15 miles from the bridge. The old town's a typical tiny Venetian outpost – attractive, formerly fortified, with a number of lovely old stone houses, a fine town square, and a mass of new houses outside the line of ancient walls. You can find accommodation

here and also at Novalja, served by the Jablanac ferry, 13 miles beyond Pag town, which you can also reach from Jablanac (Chapter 5).

A left turn before the Pag island bridge takes you to **Nin**, an extraordinarily lovely minute town with an amazing history. It was a walled Roman city, destroyed in the 6th century and later rebuilt by Slav invaders. Early Croatian kings occasionally took up residence here, and its bishop, till 828, held sway over Croatia's Christians. Nin's parish church, formerly the cathedral, was begun in the 5th or 6th century, and two other churches, Holy Cross (Sveti Križ) in Nin and St Nicholas (Sveti Nikola) nearby, are almost as old.

It was the local Bishop, the redoubtable Grgur Ninski (Gregory of Nin), who fought tooth and nail in the early 800s for his flock to be allowed to celebrate mass in their own language instead of church Glagolitic. You'll see a cast of Ivan Meštrović's powerful statue of him near the church that was once his cathedral. There's an identical but better-known copy just outside the walls of Split's old centre (Chapter 7).

The nearby tourist resorts are more modern – very modern, in fact, **Zaton** lies only 3 miles or so southwest of Nin, in a sheltered bay with an excellent sandy beach and a second, similar beach just beyond – provided you've the energy to walk there. Your accommodation here consists of self-catering apartments. You can use the entertainment and sports centres, which cater for tennis, basketball, handball, table tennis, bowling, surfboarding, water-skiing, boat hire, dancing, and occasional folklore evenings.

You must travel another 4 miles or so

to reach **Petrčane**, set in another sheltered bay with a long, curving rock and shingle beach and a tiny fishing port at its further end. There's fine modern accommodation here. One hotel has a small outdoor seawater pool, tennis, and pedalos. Punta Skala forms part of the resort. Regular buses take you into Zadar.

Huge expanses of Mediterranean pines surround both these resorts. Compared with most of Yugoslavia's coast the land's abnormally flat and fertile. For the moment the mountains are some distance away, beyond little Novigrad. The region's other main feature is its amazing collection of bare white limestone islands parallel with the shore. Nearly all are extremely long and thin, the crests of more submerged mountains. They come into sight before you reach Zadar.

Zadar's resorts

Zadar lies some six miles from Petrčane. There are hotels in the old town, on the neck of the peninsula it stands on, and in a bay to the north about 20 minutes bus ride away. You'll find the modernised Zagreb excellent for sightseeing in the town and very pleasantly located beside a flower-filled small park-like section of the town's south-facing quays. Its one lift serving five floors and 120 rooms could be a discouragement, though, to anyone inclined to impatience.

If you're staying at the Zagreb and feel like a swim you can turn left outside and wander down to the Hotel Kolovare on the peninsula's neck. It's a pleasant enough walk. There's a pebble-and-shingle beach here, as well as a nightclub and occasional folklore shows. Hotel guests can also use its swimming pool and tennis courts, and

hire surfboards. Unlike the Zagreb, the Kolovare's totally modern. Its one lift to 237 rooms on three floors may get a bit crowded at times. But the Kolovare does manage to combine a very attractive south-facing position looking out to sea with both tranquillity and nearness to the town.

Zadar's main resort accommodation, however, is in **Borik**, to the town's north. It's all contained in a pleasant, flat, spacious park-like area filled with a number of hotels of varying size and type and a fairly large self-catering village. Some hotels have swimming pools, and you've a long pebbly-shingly beach on one side of the gardens surrounding the hotels Sports and entertainment facilities include tennis, rowboat and kayak hire, dancing, nightclub, and high season folklore. You can get into Zadar by the regular public bus.

Zadar

On its squat little peninsula, pointing northwest, with a beautifully sheltered harbour on its eastern side, **Zadar** is the first of Dalmatia's superb fortified towns we come to. Rovinj, Cres, and Rab have given us a foretaste of what to expect.

Before the Romans arrived two centuries before Christ Zadar was a stronghold of the Liburni tribe, ancestors of modern Dalmatians, whose main base was at Skradin (below). Zadar's present layout was given it by the Roman Emperor Augustus, Julius Caesar's adopted son, after he'd beaten Anthony and Cleopatra at the sea battle off Actium (31 BC) largely, many historians maintain, with Liburni help. Their slim, fast war galleys were in those days the Mediterranean's best fighting ships. Actium marked Rome's defeat of

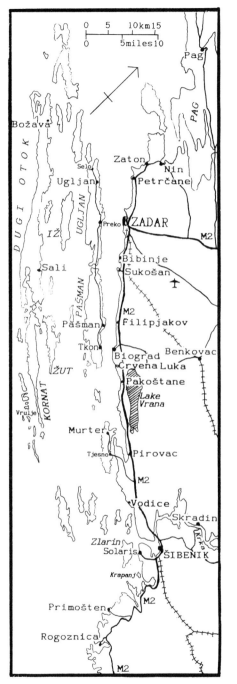

Oriental autocracy, and allowed Augustus to lay the administrative foundations of our modern Western civilisation. Maybe we owe the Dalmatians more than we realise.

Serious sightseeing in Zadar can be strenuous, especially on a really hot summer day. Despite heavy wartime bombing and much modern building there's an awful lot to see. Conducted tours show you the main sights. Useful small guidebooks in English can be bought locally. And on even a casual stroll you can hardly miss the outstanding buildings.

Excursion coaches tend to drop you on the quayside overlooking the harbour. The best starting-point however is the square just inside the Town Gate at the peninsula's base. You reach it by forking left from the main road on the peninsula's neck.

In the square itself you've a typically Venetian loggia, once used as law court and for official business, the town clock, very similar to Venice's Orologio, and some very attractive views of old stone buildings and narrow, stone-paved streets. And if you go back out through the Town Gate proper (to your left, behind you), you'll find an extremely colourful tiny yacht harbour.

Just beyond the square to your right you come to the church of St Simeon (Sveti Šimun), built at various dates from before 1190 on. St Simeon himself, wearing a silver crown, lies among finely embroidered cloths in a breathtakingly beautiful coffin made of 550 lbs of superbly worked silver above the high altar. It was completed by Francisco of Milan in 1381. Its carvings show the saint's miracles and contemporary life, including Zadar and its fortifications.

39

If you go straight towards the peninsula tip you'll come to the Roman Forum (market place and general business centre), with the huge, tall circular St Donat (Sveti Donat) church, Saint Anastasia cathedral, and the cathedral's belltower directly beyond the cleared Forum area.

St Donat dates unbelievably from the 9th century. Its architecture – a tall cylinder with three attached apses – is unusual. The church is used for concerts today. The nearby Romanesque cathedral (12th–13th centuries) incorporates much earlier Roman carvings in its decoration. The belltower beside it was restored in 1892 by T. Graham Jackson, the English architect whose three-volume study of Dalmatia's buildings is still a standard work.

Excavations in the Forum have produced a lot that's fascinating, but unfortunately there's little explanation of it available. There's a museum however on the Forum's southern side.

In the street running across the Forum's base you'll find two more churches well worth seeing – the superbly restored St Mary's, close to the Forum, and St Chrysogonus (Sveti Krševan) towards the harbour.

This doesn't by any means complete the tally of Zadar's old churches, and you'll discover a lot more as you wander round. And apart from the churches there are fine old stone mansions, old wells, remains of fortifications going back to medieval times, narrow streets, and all sorts of fascinating little oddities. Some of the postwar modern architecture also fits well with this ancient town.

Cafés and restaurants where you can buy meals and – often more important – drinks and excellent ice creams are fairly plentiful. And near the Sea Gate on the harbour side a decidedly photogenic open-air market operates from about 6 am till 12 noon. Countryfolk and islanders come in to sell their produce there. Souvenir sellers join the fun in high season.

Zadar's a natural transport hub. Smart large car-and-passenger ferries arrive here from Ancona or Rimini in Italy. Domestic services from Pula and Rijeka call here on routes connecting all the coast's main ports, together with islands such as Rab and Lošinj. The quays on the peninsula's seaward side have been extended several times into ever deeper water to provide berths for them.

Long-distance coaches ply up and down the coast and to inland towns like Zagreb from the bus station a little inland from the Land Gate. The railway station close by also provides transport to inland towns by a line built in the 1960s connecting with the colourful main Split–Zagreb route at Knin (not to be confused with Nin).

Ferries from different quayside points take you to the various offshore islands we'll be visiting soon. Scheduled domestic flights and international charters use the airport about 5 miles south of the town.

South from Zadar

The modern town has spread a long way from the little Roman and medieval city on its flat peninsula. You drive well inland through sprawling suburbs, towering flats, and smart new supermarkets to rejoin the M2 Magistrala. As you turn south you realise that the coast road for once is restfully non-hilly. It runs through a region fertile with vegetables, olives,

40

vines, and fruit. The region's wines, incidentally, are decidedly worthwhile, and very cheap.

Some six miles from Zadar you reach the turning for **Bibinje** and, after another three miles or so, one for **Sukošan**. Both are delightfully friendly, unassuming little fishing villages whose inhabitants make tourism a sideline occupation, catering impartially for Yugoslavs and foreigners alike, mainly with private-room accommodation, bars, and restaurants. The older houses in both are built of the stone that you only begin to notice when it's absent. Sukošan's beach is attractive.

Filipjakov (Philip–James), some 26 miles from Zadar, is rather similar, but boasts a modern hotel above a rocky beach on the village's edge. It takes its name from the patron saints of the church it grew up around centuries ago. The local girls are reputedly Yugoslavia's most beautiful.

Four miles beyond Filipjakov you come to **Biograd na moru** (Biograd-on-Sea, to distinguish it from other Biograds), a very colourful little town built on a conical small island joined to the mainland by a causeway. Biograd's flanked today by huge marinas – it's a major yachting base, but still a relaxed and peaceful spot. Modern hotels stand just clear of the peninsula's neck, set mostly against a background of extensive Mediterranean pines and vineyards close to a long rock-and-shingle beach, with cemented sunbathing areas. The two newer hotels have swimming pools. You can hire sailboats and rowboats from the resort's sports centre. One unusual attraction is freshwater fishing on 9-mile-long Lake Vrana inland, just a little south of Biograd, almost beside the coastal highway.

Crvena Luka (Red Bay) stands on its own, well off the road, in a delightfully sheltered small bay backed by miles of pinewoods some three miles from Biograd. It's a purely modern tourist complex, containing a hotel, extensive self-catering bungalows, supermarket, self-service restaurant, bars, hairdresser, a small marina, and a sports centre providing tennis, kayak hire, etc. The sandy beach in front of the complex is a special feature. A longer, mainly rocky beach runs round the bay.

Pakoštane, 2 miles further south, has much the same character as Crvena Luka. The resort area's next door to the tiny village and backed by the vast expanses of flat pinewoods that are typical of this section of coast.

In the 19 miles remaining before the next main town of Šibenik, on a road section that's now running further inland on slightly higher ground, you reach **Pirovac**, another unassuming fishing-and-holiday village.

Then you come to **Vodice**. Basically a fishing harbour like its neighbour, it has a 2000-visitor resort area close to it, to say nothing of thousands of private-house rooms. Here you can swim from a pebbly beach, go surfboarding, play tennis, hire rowboats or pedalos, visit the high season nightclub in one of the hotels, shop in the modern marina's duty-free shop, indulge yourself in several good ice cream parlours, or enjoy the view from the Hotel Funta's 10th-storey café. Resort and village both become busy during the holiday season. Though they lie off the main road, there's a good bus service to Šibenik every 20 minutes.

Šibenik and the Krka

Coming into **Šibenik** by road you get

tangled in a skein of traffic among mostly unattractive suburbs with even less appealing factories and workplaces. Resist the temptation to clear out again as soon as you can. Šibenik's old town centre, once you've struggled through to it, is an enchanting spot. The best approach is from the open sea via the River Krka's estuary. Your boat turns in through what looks like a gap in low cliffs and navigates for nearly two miles up the gorge-like St Anthony Channel (Sveti Ante Kanal) into a landlocked bay with the town on its opposite shore. The approach is large enough for quite big ships. Šibenik has long been an important naval base.

The old part of the town is extraordinary and extraordinarily beautiful. It's built on a steep hillside and everything, including road surfaces is built in stone. From the quay at the hill's base you climb up narrow streets and alleys that are quite as likely to consist of steps as of normal roadway. Getting vehicles into the town isn't impossible. But you have to know your way around.

Šibenik's most famous building – and deservedly so – is its amazing small cathedral. Two things about it strike you immediately – its astonishing barrel-vaulted roof, built in solid stone that must be incredibly heavy, and the frieze of 72 heads round the building's apse end. They're portraits – pretty realistic ones – of contemporary local men, women, and children. And not necessarily wholly contemporary. If you ever have to sit in on a workers council or commune council meeting or any of the other innumerable committees that run Yugoslavia (see Chapter 17) you'll find yourself facing something uncannily similar to Šibenik cathedral's frieze.

The cathedral was begun in 1431. In 1444 the famous architect–sculptor Juraj Matejević, universally known as Juraj Dalmatinac (George of Dalmatia), was put in charge. He built in Venetian Gothic till he died in 1473. Nikola Firentinac (Nicholas of Florence) then took over and completed the building in Tuscan Renaissance style. The result's astonishingly lovely. The tiny baptistery, just below the cathedral's general floor level, is full of Juraj Dalmatinac's sculpture. He was responsible for the frieze of heads as well – and for much else along this coast.

Šibenik's elegant Town Hall faces the cathedral across a beautifully paved square. Here the standard-type loggia, once open but now glazed, stands above an arcaded ground floor. The Town Hall was built in 1452, destroyed by a WWII bomb, and rebuilt exactly to its original design. You'll find the Bishop's Palace in the same square, and the Rector's Palace just below the cathedral, beside the Town Gate. The Rector had the same powers as Venice's Doge (or Duke). His official residence is now the Archaeological Museum.

When you need a cool drink and an ice cream - as you quickly will - you'll find pleasant cafés down on the quayside. It's a steep climb back.

Šibenik's extremely popular resort area, **Solaris**, lies 6 miles southwest of the town, facing the island of Zlarin (below). It caters for up to 6000 visitors in summer. You've got plenty to occupy you here - a large pebble-and-shingle beach, a sports centre that offers tennis, surfboarding, volley-ball, basket-ball, bowling, and jogging, swimming pools, dancing, speciality restaurants, a disco, weekly gala dinners, and occasional folklore evenings. The whole area's sheltered by the surrounding hills and set in well-designed gardens backed by extensive pinewoods. Solaris is extremely well-designed, and you'll find it well run too.

The Fafarinka restaurant overlooking the harbour draws lots of satisfied clients. There's a good pizzeria in Zablače village just outside Solaris. Of the several restaurants in Brodarica, a bit more than a mile south of Solaris, the best is probably the Zlatna Ribica (Little Goldfish). If you need to work up an appetite take a turn on the attractive promenade path that stretches for over a mile along the coast. One of the most popular evening spots is the Hacienda disco 15 minutes' drive from Solaris on the Vodice road. If you're travelling independently you'll find plenty of private-house accommodation in Brodarica. The only thing this little corner of the world seems to lack is a good bus service to Šibenik itself.

Šibenik's landlocked bay ends in a second narrow channel, leading into a larger bay – or lake; it's called Prokljansko Jezero (Lake Prokljan) – another section of the River Krka's estuary. The river itself tumbles down to the lake in a series of falls harnassed for centuries as fulling and corn-grinding mills. An upstream dam has altered the river's level and flow. But some of the tiny stone buildings where the falling water pounded woollen blankets or drove little cornmills have been preserved.

You'll find a popular bathing area at the lake's edge, with restaurant and bar nearby and colourful hills all round. There are campsites quite close, and a tiny hotel at **Skradin**, on the falls' northern side. The **Krka Falls** (Slapovi Krke) and bathing beach

area have been fenced in. If you drive there you're made to park your car, pay a small entrance fee, and take the public bus down to the lake.

The Romans knew Skradin as Scardona. The Liburni tribe, whose seamanship the Romans admired (and used), had their main base here.

The little fishing village of **Zlarin** stands on an island with the same name directly opposite the St Anthony Channel. Its coral industry has been revived in recent years and gives the island's Hotel Koral its name. The even smaller island of **Krapanj** holds yet another delightful old little fishing harbour as well as caves large enough to attract visitors although it's the coast's lowest inhabited island, nowhere more than 3 feet above sea level. Its inhabitants are sponge divers. A museum displays diving through the ages on Krapanj.

The Kornati Islands

We must return to Zadar and look at the remarkable islands lying immediately offshore. For the most part they're even barer of vegetation than Pag Island north of Zadar. They take their collective name, Kornati Islands, from the sizeable southernmost island, Kornat. In places Kornat isn't more than 2–300 yards wide. But it's a good 16 miles long. It is, of course, a submerged mountain crest.

If you look at the maps you'll see that the Kornati group's made up of three parallel mountain ridges. The one nearest the coast had produced the islands of Ugljan and Pašman. Then comes a line of smaller islands and islets, with names like Iž, Sit, and Žut. And then Dugi Otok (Long Island; it's 17 miles long and barely 800 yards wide at its narrowest) and Kornat, with still more jagged islands to its west.

All have bare limestone scenery as their outstanding characteristic. On Kornat, in particular, you can walk – or rather struggle – for miles over large jagged blades of sharp limestone strata. Their intimidating edges have been eroded by wind and weather into unpleasantly sharp projecting blades. It's best to avoid falling on them if you can.

The white limestone rock provides a lunar landscape background, while the wonderfully clear water at its edge almost demands that you jump in for a swim. Underwater, the coloured corals, equally bright-hued fish, and exotic shellfish are magnificent. But you'll find the region's most astonishing views are along the outer edge of Dugi Otok and the islands west of Kornat, facing across the Adriatic towards Italy. Here 200-foot high cliffs drop sheer into water 200 and sometimes 300 feet deep. It's a golden example of the "rifts" you learned about in your school geography lessons. It's where a chunk of the earth's crust just crashed inwards millions of years ago.

Not all the islands are completely bare, of course. Once, they were dotted with villages, hamlets, and isolated dwellings where people scratched livings – almost literally – by growing what they could on the land's sparse soil and by harvesting rich crops of fish from the sea. After WWII, people found they could make better livings on the mainland. The islands risked near-total depopulation. Rain washed desperately thin soil from mostly tiny, now uncultivated fields. Today tourism has begun reversing the process.

Dugi Otok's larger villages, such as

lovely little **Sali** and **Božava**, boast hotels that aren't all small. Božava, in fact offers some 400 beds, and has grown into quite a resort. If you're travelling independently you can get out there by a ferry from Zadar. It serves Dugi Otok's four main settlements. Check sailing times, however. Ferries to the outer islands are timed mostly to suit islanders carrying produce to market. They leave the islands between 4.30 and 5.30 am, and return about 4 pm.

Once on Dugi Otok you've little to do except eat, drink, enjoy the sun and the friendly local folks' attempts at conversation, swim, and follow such paths as you can find to show you more of this strange island's scenery. The peace is total. The sun's very bright, of course. It reflects almost as strongly off sea and rock as it glares and burns from above. When you get home after your first visit you'll find you seem to have scenes from the island etched permanently onto your retina.

There's no public ferry to some of the smaller islands. Nor to Kornat. But you can cross for day excursions easily enough from Zadar to **Preko** (= Beyond) on **Ugljan** island, or to **Tkon** on **Pašman** from Biograd, and explore both islands by bus. They're just yards apart and are linked by a modern bridge. In the clear water below you can make out the remains of a Roman bridge, built when land and sea levels were very different. There's a chain of villages along these islands' inner shore. The land's much flatter there, and the soil's fertile.

Kornat, the smaller islands to its west, and the southern part of Dugi Otok form the **Kornati National Park**. Excellent one-day boat tours are operated by the National Park

Authority. They give you a good idea of the scenery, and show you some marinas that have been built on these extraordinary remote islands. The area's sailing and fishing is superb.

The National Park Authority's base is at **Murter**, on the island of the same name. It lies off the mainland peninsula forming the outer side of the bay on which Pirovac stands (see above). Murter island's joined to the mainland by a small bridge at **Tjesno** – the channel's only about 30 yards wide – and local buses link **Murter** town and Tjesno with Šibenik. The island's little capital is quite charming. The main part stands on high land and flows downhill to a wonderfully peaceful and relaxed harbour that technically forms a separate hamlet called Hramina. There are places to stay at in Tjesno and Murter.

You'll find the offices of a firm called Kornatiturist in Murter too. With the help of Yugoslavia's biggest corporation, INA, they've funded the renovation of some tiny old houses on the Kornati Islands, and are offering packages to holidaymakers that include transport from and back to Murter, rent of a cottage, use of all linen and fuel, and twice-weekly provisions delivery by boat.

You can choose between a house completely on its own, one forming part of a hamlet of maybe eight or nine houses (such as Koromačna close to Kornat Island's southern tip), or one in a small village such as **Vrulje** on Kornat. Vrulje's just a line of old fishermen's cottages strung round a deep, sheltered bay.

Accommodation's very simple, but sound. One thing you can be sure of is that all your neighbours – if you have any – will be unquenchably friendly and generous.

Access

You reach the more northerly of these resorts from Zadar airport, and the more southerly from Split. The time needed to get to your hotel from the airport is never more than $1\frac{1}{2}$ hours, and often less.

Excursions

Day excursions from resorts in the Zadar region take you to Plitvice (Chapter 5), to Zadar itself, and to the Kornati Islands. From those further south you can go to Trogir and Split (Chapter 7) by coach, or to the Kornati Islands and Hvar (see Chapter 7) by boat. If you want to explore on your own you'll find local buses to the villages or Zadar or Šibenik, and ferries to the islands easy to manage and almost embarrassingly cheap.

Chapter Seven

Central Dalmatia

We've reached the Dalmatian coast's central section. It spreads to either side of the great and historic city of Split, Dalmatia's natural capital. As we get nearer the town we find high mountains coming closer to the sea. Beyond Split they flank it in places with scenery almost as spectacular as the Velebit's (Chapter 5). There are fine resorts and fine towns both north and south of the city. Another set of islands is within easy reach. They're very different in character from the Kornati we've just been considering.

The road towards Split

South of Šibenik you've a choice of roads. You can take the "high" road that goes up into the inland hills south of Šibenik and returns to the coast at Trogir (below) – the Magistrala's newest improvement. Alternatively, you can follow the older road, completed only in 1964. It runs mostly a little away from the coast through a region that isn't specially hilly or wild, though it's pretty sparsely populated. Inland from this road the terrain's higher and broken. These are the region's only surfaced roads.

In the 30 miles south of Šibenik three villages just off the old M2 are almost the only settlements you see. **Primošten**, the first of them, roughly 18 miles south, occupies yet another little conical island joined to the mainland by a narrow causeway. A church with a typical Dalmatian-Venetian belltower tops the island's cone. Three hotels, two large and one medium-sized, form Primošten's resort area on a peninsula to the town's north.

Good beaches ring the flat peninsula. Thick pinewoods cover it. The view towards the formerly-walled town, with its many white houses and red roofs, is lovely, especially when sky and sea are both deep blue. The hotels, jointly run, operate a sports centre that provides tennis, bowling, water-skiing, surfboarding, volley-ball, basket-ball, and hand-ball, and also hires boats.

You can walk to Primošten town without great effort, though you'll find the walk up to the church a little steeper than you expect. There are fewer stone buildings than elsewhere. Most of the houses belong to fishing families or to wine producers. The areas around Primošten contains innumerable vineyards, separated by little drystone walls. It's a delightful spot.

Rogoznica, some 5 miles from Primošten, occupies another causeway-linked island in a very sheltered bay. It's reached by a side road. Most of the coast is very rocky, and development's limited. You'll find rooms in private houses however.

At little **Marina**, a further 5 miles towards Split, an old castle has been turned into a restaurant and hotel.

Group of Macedonian Dancers

Novigrad, near Zadar, once a Venetian Town

Mostar in Bosnia showing signs
of its Turkish heritage

Skiing at Kranjska Gora

Marina itself lies in another well-sheltered inlet.

Trogir and the Kaštela

The loneliness of this 38-mile Magistrala section ends with a jolt as you approach **Trogir**. The Hotel Medena's two large blocks and its modern self-catering village are the first signs you see of the bustling area you're coming to.

The Medena tourist complex occupies the lower slopes of steepish hills, criss-crossed by drystone walls on their bare upper parts. You've a long pebbly beach that shelves fairly steeply a very short walk below the hotels and apartments. The water's sheltered from the open sea by Čiovo island. You can hire pedalos and boats from the sports centre, which provides also tennis and bowling. Though the airport's only about 8 miles away and in high season has flights coming in from all over Europe, noise is rarely a problem.

Tiny, gem-like Trogir is barely 5 miles off. Filled with stone buildings which at their least impressive are elegant and charming and at their best magnificent, it occupies a tiny island squeezed between the mainland and much larger Čiovo Island. It shows all the characteristics of a typical Venetian–Dalmatian town.

You cross to the island by a bridge beside the fruit market just before you reach the bus station on the mainland. If you bear a little left a narrow, straight stone-paved street will take you into the main square.

Here you've a magnificent cathedral with a superbly carved entrance on its southern side – the famous "Radovan portal", which the sculptor completed in 1240. Also in the square you'll see a typical loggia, built in its present form in 1527, a townclock, the 15th-century Town Hall, and an imposing 15th-century Venetian–Gothic mansion that was once one of the wealthy Cipiko family's homes. The tallest and most impressive of Trogir's five belltowers soars up over the cathedral's south entrance. The whole square is of course paved with the same stone that the buildings are made from. At night it reflects lights in a fairylike way.

All that's only the beginning of Trogir's delights. A surviving Town Gate leads onto the quayside close to the bridge linking Trogir to Čiovo Island. Outside it you'll see the famous "small loggia", also built in 1527, to shelter travellers who arrived after the formerly-walled little city's gates were locked. It's used today as a fish market. Tucked away in an alley beside the bigger loggia you'll find the minuscule 9th-century church of St Barbara, long disused. Many of the statues on the town clock and in Trogir's other churches were carved by Juraj Dalmatinac and Nikola Firentinac, who between them built Šibenik's exciting cathedral (Chapter 6).

The list of the tiny town's treasures is almost endless. But what you'll probably most enjoy is simply wandering through its pedestrian-sized streets and peering into the houses' tiny, flower-filled courtyards. Don't be shy about looking. The people who live there are justifiably proud of their town, and they're almost invariably delighted to show it to you – all of it. There are plenty of restaurants, cafés, and bars to feed you food, drinks, and ice cream when you need them. You'll be tempted by a lot of excellent gold and jewellery shops too.

The main road into Split, many times

re-aligned since its original construction in the 1960s, goes past the airport and does its best to avoid the line of coastal villages called the **Kaštela** (Castles). They fill the next 13 miles or so of coast on the eastern side of large Kaštela Bay (Kašteljanski Zaliv). Castles is exactly what they once were – seven small fortified points intended to deter sea raiders from attacking the long fertile plain stretching parallel with the coast behind them. They were built 500–600 years ago, at the time when Turkish attacks were most feared. Villages grew up around them.

Modern development has made them into an almost continuous built-up area. But if you poke around determinedly, or cruise along the coast in a boat, you can see at least remains of the Sućurac, Gomilica, Kambelovac, Lukšić, and Štafilić castles, and of Kaštel Stari (Old Castle) and Kaštel Novi (New Castle) between Lukšić and Štafilić. Some are very picturesque.

People swim from lots of spots along the Kaštela shore. But the village round **Kaštel Stari** (the Old Castle, built in 1476 by a member of the Cipiko family whose town house we saw in Trogir) boasts a very pleasant hotel a few minutes walk from what's just about the best beach in this area. Though traffic through the Kaštela's roads is confused and confusing, Kaštel Stari's Palace Hotel is a quiet spot to stay at, and near enough to Split if town sightseing's what you're after. The bus journey's not too long.

Salona and Split

As you reach the end of the Kaštela you see Split's shipyards on the bay's further side and hideous cement factories immediately in front, belching out horrible dust. Close to the bay's inmost point a signpost indicates the entrance to a small section of the ruins of **Salona**. Unfortunately, there's very little to be seen today, unless you hunt around and know where to look. But Salona was once a very splendid Roman town, with a theatre and baths and fine public buildings, such as were normal. What was unique in Salona was the tremendous number of 2nd and 3rd century churches and early Christian burial grounds. Most of its ruins unfortunately lie under the present Split suburb of **Solin**. It's almost impossible to locate buildings that have been excavated.

Once in Solin you're caught up in modern Split's dreadful traffic tangle. Your best bet, if you've got a car, is to park it as soon as you can and take a bus. Even local experts are driven mad by the city's parking problems. If you insist on driving into town, make for the tunnel (Tunel) under the hill Marjan that forms the high peninsula west of Split. On this route you pass on your right the superb modern stadium that's home to Split's famous football team, Hajduk (Brigand – of a Robin Hood type). If you turn left after the tunnel you'll reach the waterfront looking across to the magnificent old town. With luck – keep your fingers crossed – you'll even find somewhere to park within walking distance of the city's ancient centre. Try near the large new marina.

Split has the most extraordinary history of almost any town in the world. It started life as the Roman Emperor Diocletian's retirement palace. It stands on land sloping gently to the sea. After Diocletian's death in AD 313 it became state property and was used as a sort of VIP exiles' detention centre. But when Avars and Slavs overran the region in AD 614

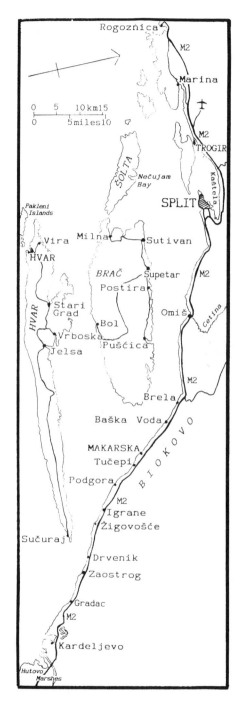

Salona's inhabitants took refuge in the palace because, as you can see even today, it was very well fortified and their town was not.

The huge square stone-built palace has been knocked about a bit in the past 1374 years. Most of it's still there, though. You can see its four fortified entrances. Three are still called Golden Gate (Zlatna Vrata), Silver Gate (Srebrna Vrata), and Iron Gate (Željezna Vrata). You can wander into the imperial audience chamber's ante-room, reached from the famous open-air Peristil (Peristyle) where the two main streets linking the four gates cross. You'll maybe meet people whose homes have been carved out of the Emperor's private apartments. These used to occupy the first floor of the palace's southern front, facing the sea.

In some ways the most impressive walk of all, you can go in through what was once the Bronze Gate, later renamed the Sea Gate, into the palace's huge storage cellars. It was only after WWII that people realised that the stone-built palace's thousands of tons weight rested on a basement composed of massive arched corridors and small open areas. These are still being cleared of nearly 2000 years' rubbish. But enough has been moved to give a good idea of what the cellars were like when first built, and to provide, in the main through passage, a pleasantly cool summer location for art and craft stalls (some of which are excellent) and a disco.

The Sea Gate once led directly to the sea. But a massive quayside, constantly broadened through recent centuries to provide deepwater ship berths and covered today with roadway, palm-filled gardens, shops, and offices, now extends in front of it.

It was renamed Titova Obala (Tito Quay) after the war. It wasn't there at all when the famous English architect, Robert Adam, spent weeks sketching Split in 1764.

If you go in through the Sea Gate and walk straight ahead past the modern jewellery and paintings and craftwork you emerge into the Peristil. The vast octagonal building on your right was designed as Diocletian's tomb, but became Split's cathedral almost as soon as the refugees from Salona had settled. It's as magnificent inside as it is out, with remains from Diocletian's day still there alongside work from every century since. That includes fine sculpture by Juraj Dalmatinac, who helped design and build Šibenik cathedral (Chapter 6).

A small Egyptian sphinx, some 3500 years old, brought from Egypt by Napoleon's troops, lies beside the entrance, and a huge belltower (13th–16th century) rises alongside. You can climb the belltower for a superb view over the town and harbour and its very modern high-rise suburbs.

Parts of the town inside the palace's 60-foot-high walls have been refashioned into narrow stone-paved streets and centuries-old houses, themselves of considerable architectural interest and value. A very colourful open-air market caters mainly for visitors on both sides of the eastern Silver Gate (to your right as you walk into the Peristil). If you turn left and go through the western Iron Gate, you emerge into the almost equally beautiful medieval town centre at the Narodni Trg (National Square). It was built with stone from the palace.

Here you can see the lovely Gothic former Town Hall (1443), with the inescapable loggia on its ground floor.

It's an excellent Ethnographic Museum today. Over the passage leading to the Iron Gate there's a town clock very similar in style to Venice's Orologio. In Renaissance Square (Trg Preporada) a little closer to the sea (turn left) the Hrvoje Tower is the most unusual and striking feature. It was built for defence. This whole area's made from lovely white stone, street paving and all. A few modern shops and offices fill gaps where buildings have tumbled down.

The rather less attractive Marmontova ulica (Marmont Street), named after Napoleon's general who conquered Dalmatia for his Emperor, runs straight inland to close off this town section. Beyond it there's another fascinating old quarter, called Varoš. It's made up of steep, winding streets, many consisting of steps, flanked by typical and often lovely old stone houses. Several are now good restaurants. Buildings here date largely from the 17th and 18th centuries.

Apart from the Ethnographic Museum already mentioned the Meštrović Gallery, some 400 yards beyond the turning to the Marjan road tunnel (on the road's inland side), is very well worth a visit – assuming you're interested in art. No one mentions Meštrovic in British art circles today. In 1945 he was considered eminent enough to be commissioned to provide sculpture for the UN's New York headquarters. He was born in Split and worked there part of his life. The gallery contains a wide-ranging collection of his work.

If you wander about the town you'll find a tremendous amount to interest you. The markets are fascinating – the vegetable and fruit stalls operate at Titova Obala's eastern end.

Bookshops, clothes shops, and wine shops are all good. There are plenty of restaurants, bars, and coffee shops dotted throughout the town.

Two good grills that operate in the open air in summer are difficult to find unless you know them. You reach one, high on Marjan hill, by a steep stairway that starts beside the quayside as you turn towards the Marjan Hotel. The other's located right on top of the tower at the palace's southeast corner. Its tiny entrance door's hidden behind a market stall selling excellent carpets, close to where vegetable and souvenir markets join. You have to be reasonably fit and agile to negotiate the narrow stone stairway to the tower's top. The ACY marina's restaurant (beyond the Hotel Marjan – below) is also worth trying.

Of the town's hotels, the main ones are the very pleasantly renovated Bellevue, an integral part of the large, distinctly Austro-Hungarian Trg Republike (Republic Square) immediately beyond Marmont Street, and the luxurious tall modern Marjan, on the quayside much further towards the Marjan tunnel. Smaller establishments also exist. Prices, by Yugoslav levels, are a bit high.

Till the late 1960s the central parts of Split which we've described constituted almost the whole town. Today they're ringed to landward by huge agglomerations of tall flats and new commercial buildings.

Transport

While talking about Split we'd better add that it's a tremendous transport base. Its airport handles international charters from a vast range of countries, as well as international and domestic scheduled services and military flying. Domestic services include flights to several main Yugoslav towns.

In Split's harbour you'll see international cruise ships and vessels operating regular services from Venice to ports in Greece, car ferries from Ancona and Pescara on Italy's Adriatic coast, fast hydrofoils taking you to Hvar, described later in this chapter, and to Korčula island (Chapter 8). Smaller vessels of various types and sizes serve minor islands.

Departure points are spread round the quay on the harbour's southern side. You'll find the bus and railway stations here too. Buses run to all coastal points as far north as Rijeka, and south as far as Ulcinj (Chapter 9). Also to a huge range of inland towns. The main rail route takes you to Zagreb in about 7 hours, with branch lines to Šibenik and Zadar. At Zagreb you connect with Yugoslavia's main rail axis – from Italy or Austria to Ljubljana, Zagreb, Belgrade, Niš (junction for Sofia and Istanbul), Skopje, the Greek frontier at Gevgelija, and on to Thessaloniki and Athens.

There's a useful taxi stand close to the rail station, and another in the main road outside the Bellevue Hotel. Titova Obala is closed to all non-official traffic. That makes driving in the town confusing for strangers. But taxis aren't expensive and you'll find the drivers helpful.

Split to Makarska

You climb the hills as soon as you start leaving Split, and before long you're riding high above the sea through a pleasant, undulating landscape of pines, olives, and vines. After about six miles a signpost indicates **Hotel Lav** (don't worry: it means Lion Hotel). But it's more than a hotel. It's a well-organised large tourist settlement laid out on spacious hills sloping down to the sea through pinewoods and gardens. It includes a large, comfortable hotel and a village of self-catering apartments, as well as a marina, an indoor pool (closed in high season), a sizeable pebbly beach, and a spacious cemented sunbathing area, as well as the excellent Arkada restaurant.

Beyond the Lav, villages are pretty well-spaced for the next 35 miles. You're still pretty high above the sea, and the scenery's pleasant and open. Then the road descends to the harbour town of **Omiš**. Cliff-like mountains rise close to the road's inland side. If you've an hour to spare, turn up the River Cetina gorge at Omiš. It's wide enough for river, road, and riverside houses. With boats tied up along the banks, flowers in the gardens, and greenery on the enclosing hills it makes a very attractive trip.

Omiš boasts a good, fairly wide sand and shingle beach with some hotels near it. They're close to the town's busy centre however.

After another 13 miles a turning marked **Brela** takes you down through thick pinewoods to a rather different resort. There's a tiny old fishing village here at the foot of steeply sloping hills. But most people's destination is the modern hotels standing just a little above sea level. They're tucked away among the pines, with a long shingle-and-pebble beach below them that you can walk to in a few minutes. In places the beach becomes quite wide. In fact, it's considered one of Yugoslavia's best. It's clean, it shelves gently, and is ideal for family swimming. The hotels have

a good range of watersports and other facilities, as well as swimming pools.

What you'll find unusual, however, is the beach-level footpath that curves round the base of the hills. You can walk the three miles to the next resort, **Baška Voda**. This is a spot with characteristics very similar to Brela's. The steeply-sloping pinewoods, the fine, sheltered beach, the path along the coast are all there.

Driving along the M2 through the pinewoods above Baška Voda and Brela you don't realise that you're on the lower slopes of a mountain – Biokovo – which for nearly 20 miles drops steeply, if not directly into the sea then down to a small strip of more level land beside it. As you get closer to Makarska however you have clear views of Biokovo's long ridge and bare, rocky side. Its highest point, directly above Makarska, reaches over 5500 feet. You can follow the track up to it from the town if you wish.

Everyone falls in love with the old part of **Makarska**. Red roofs and grey stone buildings with vast Biokovo towering over them make an unforgettable impression. But when you add a long, peaceful seafront promenade filled with squat palms looking out onto a bay protected by two large wooded peninsulas the effect's a bit overwhelming. By Dalmatia's standards Makarska's young – barely 1000 years old. Some of the old town was destroyed during the war and some suffered in the 1962 earthquake. Modern replacement buildings are happily almost as attractive as the old, which include some fine patrician mansions. Extensive recent sprawling suburbs unfortunately aren't so appealing.

You've a choice here of hotels actually in the town, on either side of it, or on the bay's two peninsulas. Two are medium-sized. Three are large. All face the sea, and the furthest away is about 20 minutes on foot from the town centre. The main resort area extends north of the town. Here there's a beach, mainly pebbly, well over a mile long. A small beach on the southern peninsula is rather wider. You'll find Makarska on the whole a fairly quiet spot. It's well sheltered from most winds, and Biokovo and the peninsulas make up a sort of heat trap. Good excursions are possible and you can play tennis if you want. But most people seem more than happy just to laze on the beach, or by a swimming pool, or wander into the town and stroll around in the evening, or sit enjoying drinks or ice creams in the shade of palms and other trees. Some Makarska hotels make special arrangements for children.

Tučepi and the "Makarska Riviera"

They call Tučepi's vast beach "the Makarska Riviera". Though 5 miles off, it's linked to the town by a pathway close to the sea as well as by the busy Magistrala a little inland.

Three large hotels and a large self-catering village have been built above the huge, mainly pebbly beach. The Kaštelet restaurant, housed in an old building in front of the Alga Hotel, has a very good reputation. Wherever you stay, you're allowed to use the swimming pool in the main hotel. Tennis is also available, though there's no great choice of other sports. Tučepi's spectacular setting below the gaunt, long Biokovo ridge seems to be the spot's main attraction. It's extremely popular with many holidaymakers.

You'll find a few older buildings in

what's now called Tučepi. The tiny real original village however lies high on Biokovo. There's no inlet here to provide natural shelter for fishing boats and no old fishing harbour.

Five fishing villages – and a port

The five resorts spread over the next 70 miles of coast are rather different. All are based on tiny old fishing harbours which you reach by steep side roads. The Magistrala's again forced well inland, high above the sea, by Biokovo's steep slope dropping sharply to a very indented coast.

The first village we come to, **Podgora**, is also the largest. The hotels here are half hidden in vast pinewoods at the village's edge or a little beyond it. They've pleasant rocky–pebbly beaches directly in front of them. Podgora's a decidedly peaceful spot today. But during the war its excellent little harbour saw the emergence in 1942 of Yugoslavia's modern navy as part of the resistance movement (see Chapter 18). The huge broken-gull-wing monument high above the village, dominating the countryside, commemorates its birth.

The next little harbour, **Igrane**, is about the smallest – at any rate of those that have become international resorts. It offers a comfortable medium-sized hotel and some self-catering apartments, close to a pleasant rock-and-pebble beach.

Žigovošće, some three miles further on, consists of several small hamlets occupying the thickly-wooded steep slopes above a long shallow bay overlooked by Biokovo's bare stony ridge. A fine pebbly beach edges the bay. It shelves gently enough to be very suitable for children. The village's main large hotel stands a little up the slope towards the bay's southern end. It has tennis courts, an indoor pool, nightclub, and terrace dancing to live music in the season. Mainly however this is just a very quiet, beautiful spot.

A few miles beyond Žigovošće **Drvenik** uses its harbour for the car ferry that crosses to Sućuraj at the southern tip of Hvar Island, which we'll be looking at in a moment. **Zaostrog**, two miles or so further on, offers one medium-small hotel close to the village.

Gradac na moru (Gradac-on-Sea: there are other towns with the same name) boasts the newest and possibly the best-designed of this area's hotels, the Labineca. By 1989 its tennis courts and bowling alley will be in full swing, along with other facilities such as a seawater pool, and children's pool and playroom. It's setting out to make a special feature of food, with a spacious dining room and a good choice of menus for main meals. It's some 15 minutes on foot from the village's centre. It has a beach of small pebbles just below it – part of a bathing area that stretches round most of Gradac's shallow bay. Biokovo's final southern slope rise directly behind the village.

Another 8 miles or so of winding, rather hilly highway bring us to **Kardeljevo**, a sort of massive, rapidly-developing non-place. It occupies a spacious enclosed deep bay just north of the fertile marshy area at the River Neretva's mouth.

Once it was a small fishing harbour and an important wartime Partisan naval base (see Chapter 17). The wide waterfront promenade in its old centre, with palmtrees down its middle, isn't unattractive. The industrial and modern port areas being developed around the old nucleus

unfortunately are. And the town's atmosphere seems to be a complete reversal of the warm enveloping friendliness you meet everywhere else on the coast. Yugoslavs say it's because all the inhabitants have come from other places: no one "belongs" and there's no community spirit.

Whatever the cause, it's unfortunate because it's difficult to avoid Kardeljevo if you're travelling independently. It's an important junction between the long-distance coaches running up and down the coast and the postwar rail line and coaches operating inland up the Neretva valley to major centres in Bosnia–Herzegovina and beyond (see Chapter 16). Till the 1970s it was called Ploče. Then it was renamed in honour of the late Edvard Kardelj, Tito's great schoolmaster associate and confidant (see Chapter 17) – not a terribly happy move, one feels, given the respect and gratitude still felt for Kardelj.

Šolta and Brač

We need to return to Split to look at three islands lying off this section of coast. Two have popular resorts on them, and one – Hvar – is exceptionally beautiful in addition.

Looking directly out to sea from Split you find the horizon filled with the two islands of Šolta (to your right) and Brač. **Šolta** as yet has relatively little tourist development beyond hotels in Nečujam and Maslinica and private-house accommodation elsewhere. A British-run sailing school is however planned for beautifully-sheltered Nečujam Bay.

Brač claims to enjoy more sunshine than anywhere else on Yugoslavia's coast – over 2700 hours a year, or an average of almost 7½ a day. As

Dalmatian islands go, it's relatively large and wide – some 28 miles by 8. Its hills go up to 2000 feet in the south, and 1000 in the north. There are large areas of cultivation and huge areas of pinewoods on the lower ground.

It's also a sort of vast and still-living open-air museum. Apart from thriving old villages, you can find here Baroque summer homes from the 18th century, Renaissance mansions 200 years older, medieval monasteries, basilicas and sarcophaguses from the days of early Slav Christianity (9th century on), Roman remains galore, and the ruins of pre-Roman Illyrian fortifications.

The island includes a number of charming old fishing villages where you can find small hotels private-house rooms, and also an occasional small pansion or two (see Chapter 19). These include Sutivan, Splitska, and Povlja on the north coast, Sumartin in the east, and enchanting little Milna (which has a large modern yacht marina) to the west.

Several other old fishing harbours however have developed large "tourist complexes" – virtually self-contained villages. **Supetar**, on the northern coast, is one of them. It has the Hotel Kaktus and the Palma Tourist Village, set in a wooded and landscaped area at the foot of a steep, stony, scrub-covered hillside, with their own pebbly beaches, tennis courts, bowling alley, football ground, nightclub, casino, dancing, and occasional folklore performances. You can hire surfboards, boats, and bicycles here, too. Or explore the nearby harbour.

Postira is rather more modest and very quiet. There are pebbly beaches close to the hotels, and a sandy cove with shade-giving tamarisks within walking distance.

Brač's main resort however is **Bol**, in the middle of the island's south coast. Excellent new tourist accommodation has been built west of its miniature harbour, directly above magnificent beaches of tiny, brilliantly white pebbles. The beaches continue to the famous and very popular Zlatni Rat (Golden Point), where the pebble expanse broadens and runs round to the headland's further side. Self-catering apartments are also available, and a fair selection of entertainments, though peace is the resort's main characteristic.

Hvar island and town

From Bol you look seaward across a channel barely 6 miles at its narrowest to long, narrow **Hvar Island**. It's almost 45 miles long, but under 3 wide for most of its length. It boasts a superb little capital, long famous as a specially sunny holiday spot, and several other lovely fishing bases that have developed recently into extremely pleasant resorts.

The largest and most prominent of them all is the island's capital, **Hvar town**. It's an exquisitely beautiful place. Its delights include a long stone-paved town square (really a decapitated triangle), with a charming small 16th century cathedral and a typical 17th-century belltower at its further end. The town loggia faces the inmost harbour quay just outside the square, with the Venetian Orologio-style clocktower alongside. Both now form part of the Palace Hotel.

On your right as you face the cathedral you've the town arsenal and grainstore, with a large arch opening into the area where centuries ago the town's war galley was stored along with essential weapons. That was built 500 years ago. Its upper storey was adapted as an enchanting tiny theatre in 1612, making it one of Europe's oldest. It's still used for concerts and shows today. The theatre boxes date from the early 19th century.

The fort high above the town makes a wonderful viewpoint – you can walk up through fine gardens or go up in an excursion coach. It stands where there was once a pre-Roman Illyrian fortress and has parts of Hvar's old town walls still attached. There's also a restaurant here and an evening disco.

There are elegant stone-built mansions going back 500 years in the town's centre around the square. But most of Hvar's houses occupy the hill–peninsula above the arsenal. Here you can wander for hours through tiny steep stone-paved streets and alleys often much too narrow for modern vehicles, among lovely old stone-built houses.

The Palace Hotel, already mentioned, occupies a superb position right in the town's heart. It has an indoor seawater pool. The nearest beach – rocky–pebbly – is 500 yards away. You can hire kayaks and rowboats here, and if you're a guest you're given one dinner a week at the restaurant in the fort above the town, complete with a folklore display. Other hotels do the same.

The recently-modernised Slavija overlooks the small harbour bay from its eastern side, and the Delfin from the west. The other hotels – the Amfora's the largest and most popular – all lie on the more distant side of the peninsula protecting the harbour's arsenal side. You can swim in their pools or from a rock-and-pebble beach directly below them. They're very comfortable, but a bit crowded in against the hill's steep slope. One of

the town's 19th century features – it has been a resort a very long time – is a cemented path running round this peninsula just above the sea.

If you fancy rather more secluded swimming you can jump on a ferry and go in 10 minutes to one of the many **Pakleni Islands** opposite Hvar's harbour mouth.

You can explore much of the island by bus. You reach Hvar town's bus station by walking through what looks like a gap in the buildings to the cathedral's left. Buses serve the lovely villages along the island's northern side that have become much-appreciated tourist resorts, probably because of their sunny, peaceful settings, and the extraordinary atmosphere of warm hospitality and friendliness they give off. The south coast's too steep for more than very occasional tiny settlements.

Starigrad or Stari Grad as it's often spelled nowadays – it still means Old Town and is officially called Starigrad na Hvaru (Starigrad-on-Hvar) to distinguish it from our other Starigrads – is the most westerly. It's set right at the base of a large, long bay, whose flat enclosing arms are covered with woods.

Modern hotels and self-catering villages have been built fairly close to the town on the bay's two arms, mostly about a mile from the town centre. Their beaches vary considerably – from man-made to an attractive area of pebble-and-rock. But you can opt for swimming pools if you prefer. Tennis courts can be hired, but there's not a big choice of sporting facilities.

Starigrad town's crammed with historical relics you can browse among. The arcaded fishpond in what remains of a Hektorović family's summer residence is among the more unusual. Churches are plentiful, and the little town's shops, restaurants, and bars are very attractive.

Yugoslavs will tell you that the island's name, Hvar, is derived from the ancient Greek pharos, meaning lighthouse. They'll even say that the lighthouse was located at Starigrad. It's a nice legend. What we know for certain is that Greeks from the Aegean island of Paros settled in Starigrad in 385 BC, and almost immediately described themselves as Pharoi in a still-surviving inscription. There was no paper in those days of course. Important records were regularly carved on stone blocks. Greeks settled in Hvar town at about the same time.

Vrboska lies at the base of another, smaller sheltered bay about 5 miles from Starigrad. Its hotel, a half-hour's walk away in the usual pinewood setting, has a good rock-and-pebble beach almost outside it. You can enjoy surfboarding, sailing, and water-skiing here.

Jelsa completes the trio of Hvar Island's northern fishing harbour resorts. The village has the almost standard background, infinitely varied in its details, of colourful quaysides and stone-built houses, overlooked by a tall church belltower. It lies at the base of yet another deep, long inlet, with its hotels and self-catering accommodation further out on the bay's arms. There are some good restaurants along the bay's steepish eastern side.

Roads link all these villages, both to Hvar town and to Sućuraj on the island's eastern tip, where the car ferry goes to Drvenik on the mainland (if you're without a car you take the

hydrofoil from **Vira**, in a bay directly northwest of Hvar town, to Split). And, as a final comment on Hvar, if you come at the right time of year, before the summer season begins, you'll find large stretches of the island's inland hillsides covered in lavender bloom. It's an extraordinary sight, and well worth taking an island bus-ride to see. Lavender oil's a major traditional local product which you can buy almost everywhere.

Access

Access is from Split airport. It's well to Split's west. But coaches to the more southerly resorts bypass the town and make good time. If you're bound for the islands they pull in at the Split quayside after circling the crowded town centre and have you quickly on board your hydrofoil or ferry for a crossing that doesn't exceed half-an-hour. Going north from the airport to Primošten is naturally very speedy.

Excursions

Excursions available depend largely on your resort's position. From the more northerly spots, such as Primošten, the Krka Falls and Zlarin and Krapanj islands (mentioned above) are easy to reach. You can make day trips from all resorts to Split. From Split itself you can go to islands like Hvar, and also the little former Turkish fortress of Klis, only a few miles away, and the nearby Vranjača Caves. Omiš and the Cetina Gorge (described above) are popular excursion destinations from Trogir and the resorts south of Split. Trogir itself (see above) is sometimes included with visits to Split.

On one day in August each year a magnificent spectacle's offered in Sinj, a small town inland from Split. The Alka, as it's called, celebrates a successful 1715 battle against the Turks with a tremendous horseriding competition. Only members of the Alkari club take part, and they all wear magnificent old costumes.

From the most southerly resorts you can go inland up the lovely Neretva valley to the delightful former Turkish frontier town and fortress of Počitelj and on to still Turkish-looking Mostar, with its famous "Old Bridge", built in 1566 in honour of the Sultan Suleiman the Magnificent, himself one of history's great builders.

The buildings close to the river at Počitelj have been carefully restored. They include a restaurant, shops, and so on. But if you climb to the top of the hill you'll realise that the village of Turkish-style houses up above is still occupied by Muslim families who have their own Muslim school and their own mosque.

There are more mosques in Mostar. Though most are now disused (some are museums which you can visit), the Turkish bazaar area near the bridge has been lovingly restored, and its little shops sell typical Muslim craftwork. For many people this is a totally new world. Mostar's described in Chapter 16.

From the more southerly resorts you can make a full day's outing to Dubrovnik, the most magnificent of all Dalmatia's cities. It's our next chapter's central point.

Chapter Eight

Southern Dalmatia

The coastland's character changes beyond Kardeljevo and the Hutovo marshes. It becomes increasingly greener and more friendly-looking. The islands too are covered with vegetation that includes vines, sometimes olives, and many other tree species as well as the Mediterranean's usual pines, cypresses, figs, and tamarisks.

This makes an extraordinary contrast with the immediate interior. Inland you can see some of the wildest karst landscapes imaginable – huge expanses of bare white craggy limestone mountains, punctuated by occasional large valley bowls that are green and fertile. These often contain a central small town and several surrounding villages. Streams may drain into them. The Yugoslav word "polje" is used to indicate these karst valley-bowls.

The coast, in contrast, has a settled, well-heeled, comfortable feeling, and the superb old city of Dubrovnik dominates it. The bulk of the region, in fact, was for centuries ruled by the Republic of Dubrovnik, constantly struggling for independence from Venice, who dominated the sea, and from the Turks, whose frontier lay only a few miles inland.

The Hutovo Marshes and Klek–Neum

The **Hutovo Marshes** consist of silt brought down by the fast-flowing Neretva from Bosnia–Herzegovina's mountains. They cover a pretty vast area, crossed today by a huge bridge and the modern road. Till a few years ago you had to drive all the way inland to Metković, the River Neretva's busy port, nearly 20 miles from open sea.

The marshland's fertile and colourful, producing rich crops of vegetables and fruit of many sorts. If you drive to Metković you'll find the route lined with stalls selling whatever fruit's in season. Roads inside the marshy area are scarce. Farmers make their way about in boats. You get a few good views from the north-bound approach road, but see relatively little going south. The only outsiders who ever get to know these marshes properly are people who can afford to shoot wild duck and other game here.

Beyond the craggy hills closing in the marshes' southern side you pass long, narrow Klek–Neum Bay. It has **Klek** village near its mouth and **Neum**, just off the road, by its base. This is a wonderfully sheltered position. Several hotels and clusters of self-catering apartments close to these villages are built on slopes that give you magnificent views across the tiny tongue of land shutting in the bay to vast, wooded Pelješac peninsula beyond. Its mountains, with only scrub above the tree-line, rise over 3000 feet.

There's a pebbly beach along the

Klek–Neum shore. Tennis, sailing, surfboarding, a bowling alley, and in one hotel even billiards is available, with live music, discos, and occasional folklore in the evenings. You can enjoy a number of bars and restaurants in the mainly modern villages.

Neum has the distinction of being the only point along the coast between Portorož (Chapter 4) and the Sutorina Hills south of Dubrovnik (see below) that doesn't belong to Croatia. Bosnia–Herzegovina has a 12-mile corridor to the sea here. The road and rail link to Kardeljevo functions as its real trade outlet however.

The Pelješac peninsula

Coming from the north, you can cross to Pelješac by a ferry from Kardeljevo. You land at **Trpanj**. It's a quiet village at the bottom of a long, richly-wooded valley. Trpanj has two or three small hotels. A fair number of houses offer private rooms. Buses connect with the ferries to take you to Pelješac's main resort, Orebič.

On the way you get a good idea of Pelješac's extraordinary contrasts. You start in the valley's dense woods and rich cultivation. Then you join the main road from the peninsula's base and soon round a bare, cliff-like mountain high above the sea, with superb views over nearby Korčula island. It was even more exciting when the road consisted only of pebbles a good foot deep. You were never quite sure when the stones would just roll you over the cliff's edge.

It's a 5-mile downhill run to **Orebić**, a good 35 miles from the peninsula's base and 10 from its tip. The little town has grown enormously in the last 20 years. But in one respect it's still unique.

In most of Dalmatia there are few old houses between ordinary folk's stone cottages and noble families' often superbly ornate homes and summer residences. Orebić however has a notable collection of tall 19th century middle-class homes, not built wholly in stone. They belonged to sea captains and their families. The town not only used to produce a disproportionate tally of master mariners; it was also a favourite retirement spot.

One of these houses is by special arrangement opened to visitors, and is well worth seeing – especially the kitchen on the 3rd floor under the roof. It's located there because the builders reckoned (in the days before gas and electricity) that a fire started by a charcoal stove might take the roof off, but would hopefully leave the rest of the house untouched.

Orebić also possesses a charming small maritime museum. The old village is grouped around its tiny harbour. Frequent passenger ferries cross from here to Korčula town (see below). The car ferries land in a bay east of it. Unless you're prepared for tough walking under a maybe blazing sun be patient and wait for a passenger ferry.

Orebić's hotels are located in pinewoods strung out westward above the shore – a pleasant 10–20 minute shaded walk from the village. The oldest of them actually dates from pre-war days, and was used as a wartime stable. But it has been excellently renovated. The others are modern.

The beach below them is mainly pebbly. But there are one or two odd little patches of firm sand underwater. These are specially attractive for children. They and their parents can lie on the grass backing the beach, half-shaded under pines, and also hunt

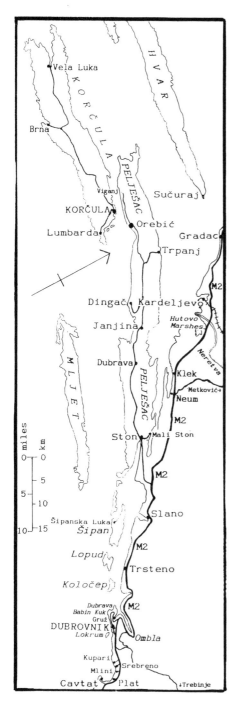

out miniature rocky coves on either side of the main beach. Windsurfing, bicycle hire, tennis, a fortnightly folklore evening, and dancing every high-season evening to live music on the Rathaneum terrace are regular for the Orebić hotels. There's also a private ferry with fixed departure times from the hotels' own pier to Korčula.

You'll find good shops and a supermarket close to the village's centre. And if you carry on along the promenade beside the sea you come to several worthwhile restaurants. If you want real Yugoslav food, choose one that's full of Yugoslav customers.

If you're energetic you can walk to the old monastery high above the village, and even continue towards the peninsula's tip by a rough footpath that passes a number of old farms, some now abandoned. It's a mostly bare landscape at this height. Elsewhere, you'll find very attractive old villages, with delightful stone houses, old churches, and occasional monasteries, scattered over Pelješac's 43-mile length – places like **Janjina** and **Dubrava** on the main road, as well as Trpanj on the northern shore, and others on dead-end roads of their own.

Dingač, on Pelješac's southern shore about 15 miles east of Orebić, gives its name to the heavy red wine produced there. It's standard drinking for miles around. You can visit the winery. But Dingač isn't the region's only wine. Plavac is also popular. Plav means blue. The dark red wine shows a blueish tinge when you hold your glass to the light. Pelješac's vineyards have been famous for centuries.

Tiny **Ston**, right at the peninsula's base, is worth a visit. The town's fortified, and the peninsula's narrow

65

enough here for its walls to be continued over a steep, rocky hill right across to a fortress on the further shore, in the village known as **Mali Ston** (Little Ston). The walls' purpose was to deter land attacks on Dubrovnik's territory.

Mali Ston's minute old centre inside its walls is totally unspoilt and unspoilable. You'll find friendly shops and bars here. Still water in the bay it faces is ideal for oyster-breeding. There are extensive oyster beds here. A restaurant a little before the village serves local oysters in season. There are fascinating saltpans in the bay on the peninsula's other side.

Korčula town and Korčula island

In Orebić the ancient walled town of **Korčula** catches your eye all the time. Though tiny, its beauty puts it in the same class as Split and even Dubrovnik. It stands on a tiny hill peninsula jutting out into the narrow Pelješac Channel. Part of its fortifications are still standing, notably the fine Land Gate and several towers. A 4th century BC Greek inscription, carved on locally-quarried stone, calls it a "stone-built city", which it still decidedly is. The chances are that its fish-skeleton layout – a main street backbone with streets slanting off it like fishbones (good protection against strong northern winds) – is an example of ancient Greek town-planning.

Whether that's true or not, you'll find the town exceptionally attractive. The church that was built as the cathedral of St Mark occupies the main part of the tiny town square at the peninsula's highest point (after 500 years Korčula stopped having a bishop in 1828). The former Bishop's Palace lies to your right as you face its entrance. Today this houses a first-rate small museum containing the former cathedral's unusually rich treasure and other lovely things.

If you come through the Land Gate you'll find an elegant little Town Hall in the tiny square just inside the gate. Its colonnaded ground floor dates from 1525 and its upper floor from 1866. The tiny 14th-century All Saints church close to the Land Gate has a well-known collection of icons in its adjoining fraternity hall.

One of the houses down a steep narrow lane on the main street's southern side has long been occupied by a family called Polo. It's advertised as "Marco Polo's home". The claim has advanced over the years from plain "Polo family house". Polos have certainly lived in the house for centuries. But there's no proof that the great 13th-century explorer came from Korčula. Equally, there's no reason why he shouldn't have been born here. Huge numbers of Venice's sea captains came from the Yugoslav coast.

If you wander through the streets immediately outside the Land Gate you'll find they're full of fine, small 16th and 17th-century mansions. One of them was presented to Brigadier Sir Fitzroy Maclean by Marshal Tito at the end of the war, in recognition of the help he gave Yugoslavia after being parachuted to join the Partisans in 1943 as Churchill's personal representative. Sir Fitzroy and Lady Maclean still divide their time between Korčula and their Scottish home.

In addition to all its fine buildings Korčula can also boast an ancient dramatic sword dance of a type once fairly common throughout the Mediterranean and elsewhere. It's called the Moreška. That means "Moorish" – which is precisely what a lot of people believe is the meaning of our own "Morris" dances.

The Moreška's outstandingly exciting. Each dancer uses two swords, one for attack and one for defence. Some figures are fast and furious and it's easy for dancers to get slight blows on the head. In fact, it's rare for a performance not to draw blood. When the Moreška dancers came to London in 1966 and danced in the Albert Hall they brought three reserves and their own doctor.

In days gone by performances were limited to 29 July each year. Now you can see it in Korčula every summer Thursday evening at sunset – its's far too strenuous to be even thought of till sundown.

The hotels and self-catering complexes round Korčula town are all inevitably a little way from the tiny old walled city – apart from the long-established little Korčula Hotel at the quayside where the steamers still call that were once the coast's only form of transport. It's some way from a beach, and has no swimming pool. But it's fine for sightseeing in the town.

Most of the rest are perched among pinewoods at least a little way up slopes above beaches that are mostly rocky and pebbly. The majority have swimming pools and good sports facilities, as well as excellent folklore performances provided mainly by a local school led by their enterprising headmaster.

Surfboarding's specially popular in the sheltered waters off Korčula town.

Nearly 30 miles away, almost at Korčula island's further end, the large village – or is it a tiny town? – of **Vela Luka** lies at a long bay's deepest

point (Vela Luka means Big Harbour). There's a hotel right on the shore opposite the village. It's a delightfully quiet spot, with a rock beach directly below the hotel and a shuttle launch service to the town and its shops and bars and restaurants.

The hotel makes a point of using local "klapa" singers to entertain guests regularly in summer – and very good they are. Impromptu singing by "klape" (groups) in up to six parts is normal in "urban" Dalmatia. Out of Vela Luka's 4000 inhabitants over 40 groups meet regularly to sing just for pleasure. Formal rehearsals are held only by groups entering competitions. You'll never know what you're missing till you hear a good klapa. Every Dalmatian seems to know scores of songs. It's quite possible for an impromptu session to last right through the night without any number being repeated.

Lumbarda, right at Korčula island's further end, only about 8 miles from Korčula town, caters also for tourists in a slightly muted way. It's a quiet little typically Dalmatian harbour village, famous mainly for the nearby quarries. The stone that built both Korčula and Dubrovnik was quarried here.

On Korčula's south coast little **Brna** lies in a quiet bay ringed by thickly-wooded mountains. The hotel's perched right on the rocky shore. But there's a good sandy beach reasonably close. Tennis, bowling, surfboarding, and boat hire are available. Public buses operate to Korčula town (21 miles) and Vela Luka (12 miles). The region round about produces the excellent light white Pošip wine.

The road to Dubrovnik

We must go back to the Magistrala

M2 coastal highway a bit beyond Ston. It's under 10 miles to the much-appreciated little resort of **Slano**. It lies deep in a sheltered bay that the road winds round. Two splendid modern hotels have been built beside the shore close to a tiny, colourful medieval fishing village. They enjoy a wonderfully peaceful position, but offer all the activities anyone could want – tennis, surfboarding, cycling, pedalos, basket-ball, hand-ball and, of course, a disco. Slano's beach and setting suit children well.

After coming down close to the sea at Slano the M2 winds south again on hills above the sea. At **Trsteno**, some 18 miles from Dubrovnik, you can visit one of the magnificent summer homes Dubrovnik nobles built for themselves in bygone centuries. In this case the data was 1502. Later Gučetić family members improved on both house and park. Statues, fountains, palms, camphor trees, giant planes, and all sorts of exotic plants fill the park. The house contains mainly 18th and 19th-century furniture. The painter Titian and the poet Byron were among the famous people who were guests here in the past. Renovation after wartime damage and postwar neglect is almost complete. There are also other aristocratic summer homes in the village.

A few more miles brings us to **Orašac**, with the old village inland over half-a-mile from the sea and the new resort area right on the coast. Accommodation consists of a carefully-planned "holiday village" of self-catering apartments, built in blocks round a central reception area. Each block has shops on the ground floor. Together, they provide everything visitors can need, including several types of restaurant.

Past Orašac the road winds inland round another mile-long bay. After 3 further miles you find yourself heading inland along the northern shore of what seems an enormously long, narrow inlet. It's a very lovely scene. Tall cypresses, willows, and fruit trees grow beside the water. The fields look green – which isn't always normal in these latitudes. The water shows greeny-blue instead of the deep blue of the open sea. A huge number of new-looking houses are dotted about, with some very fine older buildings among them, especially on the inlet's further side. Large marinas are much in evidence.

In actual fact, this isn't a sea inlet. It's the estuary of a large river that flows from the base of a cliff 1000 feet high right at the "inlet's" end. It's the continuation of the River Trebišnjica, which disappears into ground not far from the village of Hutovo, close to the marshes, and 30 miles from this spot where it reappears (a not unusual event in limestone regions). Officially, the inlet's name is Rijeka Dubrovačka – Dubrovnik River. But everyone calls the spot the **Ombla**. Unfortunately, the river's actual source at the cliff base is now screened off. It used to be a very impressive sight.

After a hairpin turn at the inlet's end you pass the old village of **Komolac**, where centuries ago noble Dubrovnik families built themselves impressive summer homes. If you keep to the road just above sea level you come to Dubrovnik's modern harbour in the former village of Gruž. But we must go back to look at some offshore islands.

Mljet, Šipan, Lopud, and Koločep

The island of **Mljet** lies south of

Pelješac's landward half. Clumped with hills, it's thickly forested and protected as a National Park. Roman remains and earlier relics are common here. For sheer peace it's hard to beat the island's Melita Hotel – a beautifully converted 12th-century Benedictine abbey with 40 rooms, standing in the middle of what's called the Great Lake but is actually a bay linked to the sea by a very tiny channel. There's a modern 312-bed hotel on the seashore not far away. The mountainous island's peacefulness is its main appeal, along with its heavily-wooded setting.

Tiny Šipan, Lopud, and Koločep are collectively known as the Elaphitic Islands (Elafitski Otoci). They too were once part of the region ruled by Dubrovnik. And wealthy Dubrovnik families built fine summer homes here too.

The largest, **Šipan**, lies south of Slano. Its village capital, Šipanska Luka (Šipan Bay), looks out onto yet another well-sheltered bay and boasts a medium-sized modest modern hotel above a rock-and-pebble beach. If you fancy yourself as an amateur archaeologist you can have the time of your life exploring Šipan. Several fine old mansions are in ruins. So are 15 of the island's 30 churches, the earliest going back 900 years, built before even Romanesque architecture had reached this part of the world. At the other end of the island, in Sudjuradj, you can see two fortified summer houses very similar to the Kaštela north of Split (Chapter 7).

Lopud island's capital is also called Lopud. Its little bay is protected by forts on each enclosing peninsula, with a rock-and-shingle beach below the town at its base. Remains of medieval fortifications can still be seen. Three hotels are all situated near the town, with pleasant beaches near them. It's a typically peaceful island setting.

Closest to Dubrovnik and also tiniest of the Islands, **Koločep** boasts only two settlements, Upper Village and Lower Village (Gornji Selo and Donji Selo). Churches and church remains are a lot more numerous, and the earliest, as on Šipan, is 1000 years old.

But Donji Selo can claim what's an almost greater rarity in Dalmatia – a sandy beach that's excellent for children. You can hire surfboards and pedalos, and dance to live music in the evenings in season. The place's main appeal however is, again, just peacefulness.

Alone of these islands, Koločep's served by scheduled-departure launches which allow day visits both to and from Dubrovnik. Journey time's 40 minutes. Companies operating packages to the other Elaphitic Islands take passengers out and back by special launches, and also run special excursion boats to Dubrovnik. Independent mortals have to go out by the locals' own afternoon service and return around dawn a day or more later (see Excursions, Chapter 7).

Dubrovnik's resorts

We left the M2 Magistrala at the approach to **Gruž**, Dubrovnik's modern port. The sudden burst of tatty industrial buildings and shipyards makes a sorry contrast with the beauties of the Ombla and Komolac. But it doesn't last too long. You soon reach the harbour proper, with a fine mixture of obviously old buildings, including even a monastery, on the wide quay's inner side, and smart modern ships and buildings at the water's edge. Ferries from here go to Bari and Ancona in Italy and to Corfu and Igoumenitsa in Greece, as well as up and down the Yugoslav coast and out to offshore islands.

As you come to the harbour's further end you're very aware of shops and supermarkets, heavy traffic, and all the trappings of modern urban life. It's clearly a very busy spot – and very different from the glories of ancient Dubrovnik you've heard about.

We'd better explain the layout of the resort that the brochures call "Dubrovnik". It's really something like 11 resorts strung out over 18 miles or more of coastline (less as crows fly). There's only one tiny hotel actually inside the magnificent walled city and one 200 yards or so from one of its gates. Four more are close enough to walk to the town from them – provided you're reasonably fit and energetic. The rest are totally separate.

Starting in the west, the **Babin Kuk/Dubrava** tourist complexes going all round the tip of the broad peninsula sheltering Gruž harbour are among the newest. They're really a separate settlement. They've been very carefully and thoroughly planned to provide pleasant and very green settings and all possible facilities, including a fine sports centre. The beaches however – mostly rocky – face the open sea, so that surfboarding and other watersports are liable to be limited. Regular public buses take you cheaply and reasonably comfortably into Dubrovnik. Queuing to get back, with the bus possibly very crowded for the first part of the journey, isn't quite so comfortable. But there's nothing unpleasant about it.

The next hotel area's in sheltered **Lapad Bay**, known also as Sumartin Bay. It lies east of the Babin Kuk-

Dubrava region. Some of the Lapad hotels are rather older, though well modernised. Several have rocky beaches below them. From others you use the long-established, well-organised, large rock-and-shingle public beach. It has a pleasant public park beside it. The bay's whole setting betokens more leisured days. Development here was well under way in the 1930s.

In and near Gruž, a little closer to the Old Town, hotels are very mixed. One fully modernised Victorian building overlooks the harbour. Another's built on the peninsula neck's outer edge looking south to the open sea. One from the late 1960s looks out onto the harbour from a different spot.

Closer still, several hotels have been built in recent years in Dance Bay and Pile Bay on the steep seaward side of the road climbing over the hill between Gruž and Dubrovnik (more accurately, the roads: a very confusing one-way system's essential today). They include some officially graded de luxe, as well as the old Imperial a few hundred yards outside the town's Pile Gate. The little Dubravka's the only hotel inside the walls, but several very comfortable establishments are stretched out along the increasingly steep shore on the Ploče side.

Kupari, Srebreno, and Mlini, some miles beyond Dubrovnik proper, are often treated as part of the city. They're really some 5 miles away. We deal with them separately.

But before we continue with resorts east of Dubrovnik proper we must look at the remarkable town that was this area's original magnet. And before we do that we'd better ask how independent travellers can cope with booking accommodation after they arrive in Dubrovnik.

70

Independent bookings

You can make bookings through the Tourist Office, located on your right just inside the Pile Gate. But first you've got to get there from the harbour at Gruž or from the bus station (autobusni kolodvor) close to it. You can take a taxi, of course, though they're relatively expensive in Dubrovnik (almost the only Yugoslav town where that's the case). Or you can catch a local bus – from outside the bus station: only long-distance services start from inside it. Your destination's Pile.

What sort of accommodation do you want? Hotels are virtually all closely geared to package tours. Individuals not only pay much more than group travellers, they also get less attention. A room in a private house may be the answer. If you want one inside the city walls – well, it's quite possible. Most of these rooms are extremely attractively situated, and very reasonable in price. You can normally book them only through the Tourist Office.

There are also lots of rooms to be had in Gruž, in modern houses as well as old, and you make your bookings from the women you find outside the bus station or on the quayside. You won't be ripped off. To begin with it's not a Yugoslav custom. And in any case all accommodation's graded and prices officially fixed.

Gruž village climbs steeply up Mount Srđ from the harbour. If you stay here you'll discover a maze of steep streets, alleys, and passageways. Many consist just of steps, and an extraordinary tangle of ancient stone-paved paths thread their way right to Dubrovnik. They pass all sorts of attractive old buildings that you'd never otherwise realise were there.

Dubrovnik: the old town

To an extraordinary extent **Dubrovnik** has changed little since the great earthquake of 1667. The massive walls and defensive towers, the houses, and the main buildings are all still there. The Onofrio Great Fountain, just inside Pile Gate, looks just as it did when it first brought water all the way from a spring close to the Ombla in 1437 to give Dubrovnik its first public water supply. And the water, incidentally, is still extremely clean, cool, and thirst-quenching. Lots of visitors produce plastic cups and bottles and drink from it.

As you can imagine, this astonishing little place has an equally amazing history. Extant documents tell us that some time before AD 667 (when its old name Ragusium first appears) it was occupied by refugees from a town called Epidaurum (which may have been Cavtat: see below) after their settlement was overrun by Slav and Avar invaders – much as Salona's inhabitants moved to Diocletian's Palace in Split (Chapter 7).

We know that by 972 there was a fortress where the Pile Gate now stands. The name Dubrovnik was in use by 1189, though the town continued to be known also as Ragusa (especially in Italian) right down to recent years. The importance it once held is shown by our regular use of the word "argosy" to mean a particularly large and wealthy merchant vessel. The word's simply another version of Ragusa. Fighting off Byzantines, Saracens, Macedonians, Crusaders, Hungarians, Venetians, Turks, and others, and subject to Venice for only the years 1205–1358, it remained an independent republic until 1808, when Napoleon abolished its constitution.

In 1815 the Congress of Vienna, called to reorganise Europe after Napoleon's final defeat, refused even to hear a delegation from the little republic. It was given to Austria instead, and made part of the Austro-Hungarian empire's Province of Croatia. In 1918 it was included in the Kingdom of Yugoslavia. Today it's part of the Republic of Croatia (see Chapter 18 for general Yugoslav history).

At the height of its power, from about AD 1000 to 1800, Dubrovnik was a trading rival of pre-eminent Venice. It ruled the coast from the present Croatia–Montenegro boundary (see below) to Klek, described earlier in this chapter. Its ships traded widely throughout the Mediterranean: it was a Ragusan carrack that told Nelson where to find the French fleet off Trafalgar in 1805. Its merchants had reps and agents in ports and inland towns as far away as Constantinople. The fact that the official frontier between Venice and Turkey lay at the top of the cliff above the Ombla and along the nearby hills' crests made no difference.

The city's constitution was modelled on Venice's. Effective power was held by the aristocratic Senate. Every son of a noble house automatically became a member at the age of 18. The Senate elected a Rector, who acted as Head of State for just a month and couldn't be re-elected for two years. They also elected a Minor Council to advise him about day-to-day administration.

In matters of health, hygiene, education, town planning, and the like the tiny town was amazingly advanced. Manchester and most British towns had nothing like the 7-mile aqueduct (with only a 30-foot fall over its entire length) and the impressive fountain built by the South Italian Onofrio de la Cava till 400 years after Dubrovnik's Great Fountain began operating. In Europe only Amsterdam has been town-planned as Dubrovnik was since its earliest beginnings.

By the end of the 1300s Dubrovnik already maintained an effective quarantine station for seamen, travellers, and cargoes waiting to enter the town. The reconstructed lazaretti just outside the Ploče Gate date from 1627. Ships' crews and caravan merchants stayed in their ground-level buildings, used today as attractive boutiques, for 40 days before being allowed into the town. Their goods were stored in the basements. As for education, that was already well advanced in the 15th and 16th centuries. In the 18th century the physicist and philosopher Ruđer Bošković of Dubrovnik was elected a Fellow of the Royal Society, still considered among the highest accolades available to scientists.

What you see in the town today reflects its former prosperity and proud history. Go in through either the Pile (western) or Ploče (eastern) Gate, and thread your way into the long rectangular Placa, the Town Square.

The white stone of buildings and paving shines like marble. Ordinary houses are superb, public buildings magnificent. The vast Onofrio Fountain stands to your right as you come through the final Pile fortifications. The Franciscan Monastery on your left (you can go straight in) contains Europe's oldest still-operating pharmacy. It provides modern medicaments today and is used by the locals just as you use your prescribing chemist – and it has been doing just that since 1317. It retains its magnificent centuries-old appearance however, with a breathtaking array of superb old chemist's jars and furniture.

The pharmacists incidentally mostly speak English and can be very helpful with minor problems. They also sell a face cream of their own devising, that's said to be excellent – and is certainly cheap.

If you continue down the Placa's polished paving you'll see directly ahead a variation on the Venetian-style Campanile belltower. It's combined with the town-clock Orologio. The Column of Orlando, with the statue of a knight to one side and a flagpole on top, stands in front of it. We know Orlando as Roland, leader of a gallant group of knights said to have attacked Arab invaders at Roncesvalles in the Pyrenees in AD 788. Modern researchers suggest it wasn't Arab invaders they attacked, but Charlemagne's Christian army. Whatever the truth, Roland-Orlando became freedom's symbol not only to Dubrovnik but also to much of Europe. It was here the republic's laws were announced. The present column's "new". It replaced the original in 1418.

The lovely building on the column's left at the Placa's end is the former Customs House, the Sponza. It's open to the public and used sometimes for concerts and exhibitions. Above the gateway leading to the Ploče Gate, between the Sponza and the clocktower, you'll see a small terrace. From 1469 on it housed the town's signal bell, summoning council meetings and ringing the alarm at moments of danger. The Town Guard occupied the charming building on the belltower's right, and the large café next door was once the town's

arsenal. It had room for four war galleys. You can still see three of its arches from the harbour side. The Onofrio Small Fountain's on its Placa side.

The church to Orlando's right is dedicated to St Blaise (Sveti Vlaho), Dubrovnik's patron saint (you'll see his statue over the Pile Gate and in lots of other places). It was designed by an Italian architect after the original church was destroyed by the 1667 earthquake and ensuing fire. However, you can still see, above the high altar, the lovely 15th-century silver-gilt statue of St Blaise holding a model of Dubrovnik as it was before the earthquake. Miraculously, it survived earthquake and fire. The church owns many fine paintings, too.

The Rector's Palace, the Dvor, stands diagonally opposite St Blaise's church, with the modern – well, 1882 – Town Hall between it and the former arsenal. The Dvor's beautiful colonnaded vestibule, rebuilt after the earthquake, is much appreciated as a shaded resting-place for tiring sightseers. It's a very lovely bit of work.

If you go into the main courtyard, just inside the huge entrance doors, you'll get a good idea of Dubrovnik's wealth in the days of its power. There's a small charge for admission, which entitles you to see also all the beautifully-furnished and beautifully-decorated public rooms. Chamber music's performed in the entrance courtyard during Dubrovnik's summer festival.

Dubrovnik's cathedral, diagonally opposite the Dvor, was also built after the earthquake and fire. It replaced a much older church, built largely with money donated by Richard Coeur de

Lion (Richard I of England) as a thank-offering for his survival after a shipwreck on the island of Lokrum (see below) while on his way to the Holy Land. A grand, ornate, Baroque building, it looks a bit out of place. It was designed by an Italian architect who never even visited Dubrovnik. The Bishop's Palace stands opposite the cathedral.

If you go through the little street opposite the Dvor you come to Gundulić Square (Gundulićevo Poljana), named after the republic's greatest poet. His statue stands in the middle, surrounded by market stalls where you can buy deliciously fresh fruit up to about midday.

Facing you as you come into the square is the elegant little Hotel Dubravka. To your left a grand stairway, where children play and tourists eat their picnics, leads up to Bosković Square, the fine Jesuit Church, and the adjoining Collegium Ragusinum, Dubrovnik's oldest seat of higher learning. If you go along Strossmayer Street (Štrosmajerova ulica: just before the top of the stairs) you come to Rupe (the Rocks). It was the city's ancient emergency grain store and is now a museum.

Back in the Placa (known to locals as Stradun – the street) you can go through the archway beside the clocktower and follow the winding route to the Ploče Gate. You pass several lovely tiny chapels, no longer used for religious services. One sells excellent pastries and ice creams (but maybe by the time you read this it will have gone back to being a fashion boutique).

On the way you'll also see an invitingly magnificent short stairway leading to the Dominican monastery's entrance. Its cloisters are particularly attractive.

A little beyond the final Ploče fortifications you'll find the view of the Old Harbour and the three arches leading into the former arsenal particularly fine. You can get into the harbour area from beside the Town Guardhouse. Lots of excursions start from the harbour. It's also where launches arrive from resorts east of Dubrovnik (see below).

You'll inevitably want to explore the fairylike steep narrow streets on the Placa's north (Sponza side). Many are colourful with hanging flower baskets and climbing vines, and all are steep enough to consist partly of steps – all, of course, built of the same magnificent white stone. You'll find plenty of restaurants here, especially in the street called Prijeko, parallel with the Placa. It got its name, which means "Beyond", from the fact that in about AD 700 the part of Dubrovnik on the Placa's other side where refugees from Epidaurum settled was an island. When the tiny town expanded by filling in the dividing channel the new area was called "Beyond".

You'll also want to explore the flat streets of the town's original area. They're less exciting. But they've pleasant shops and restaurants and bars, and you'll find a particularly good and cheap self-service restaurant close to Gundulić Square. No one speaks English there. You just point and hold up fingers (carefully!) for the number of portions you want. Everything's complicated by your having to pay in advance and hand over a chit for the food and drink you take. But the place has coped cheerfully with polyglot tourists for years.

If you dive into the less attractive-looking (and smelling) arched and stepped alleys beyond the cathedral and make your way to the walls you'll be able to discover a little postern gate that takes you through the vast walls onto rocks from which you can dive into 20 feet or so of clear blue sea. Locals use the spot a lot.

There's plenty more you can do in old Dubrovnik. South of the main bus stops at Pile (to your right as you arrive) there's a small park and what's almost a separate tiny village beyond it. Beyond that there are two tiny beaches and yacht harbours separated by a high, rocky peninsula with Fort Lovrjenac (Fort St Lawrence) perched on top. You can climb up right into the fort.

A travel firm's Dubrovnik headquarters occupies a superb patrician mansion close to the Pile Gate. It's worth going in just to look round. And just beyond the Ploče Gate you'll find signs directing you to the cableway that takes you to the top of Mount Srđ, the 1500-foot hill towering over the town. The view from the top's magnificent.

Frequent launches leave from the Old Harbour to the forested island of Lokrum, only a few minutes away. It's where Richard I is said to have been shipwrecked 800 years ago. There are pleasant, shaded paths, and a restaurant and hotel.

Finally (you're into about your third day of sightseeing by now, especially if you've stopped to poke about among all the fascinating things not mentioned here), it's criminal for anyone, unless they're incapable of walking more than a few hundred yards, not to make the circuit of the town on top of the walls. The constantly-changing views of red roofs, the extraordinary chimneys designed to counter downdrafts, the climbing vines and rooftop flowers, the

surprising number of gardens concealed behind high walls, the view into monastery cloisters – including St Catherine's near the Pile Gate, used today as a restaurant – and, above all, the stupendous view down the Placa's whole length to the clocktower and the mountains beyond – these aren't things you (or your camera) will ever forget. You can get drinks at a little stall on the southern side. The main entrances to the wall are close to the Pile and Ploče Gates.

When you reach the Minčeta Tower, the largest tower of all, at the town's northwestern corner, bear in mind that it was designed by Juraj Dalmatinac, the sculptor responsible for much of Šibenik cathedral and for magnificent carvings in Split cathedral and innumerable other places in Dalmatia. It's only in about the last century that we've taken to making useful things ugly and persuading ourselves that artists aren't practical.

If you see only a fraction of what's mentioned here – and that's only a fraction of everything worth seeing (we've not mentioned the old libraries and paintings and archives, for instance) – you'll understand why UNESCO lists Dubrovnik as part of the whole world's heritage.

Kupari, Srebreno, and Mlini

Beyond Dubrovnik the Magistrala climbs continuously, first past the Argentina and Excelsior hotels and scores of new holiday homes, and then into open country, with a long, steep slope to the sea. Not so many years ago Kupari, Srebreno, and Mlini were tiny hamlets at the foot of this slope, each reached by a separate road. Kupari was an army holiday centre. Srebreno had a tiny hotel, and you walked along the beach to Mlini, where there was a pleasant pre-war hotel. Today the area has been pretty heavily built up to make three popular resorts.

Kupari enjoys a spacious, park-like, flat layout, with hotels, restaurants, and shops standing back from the sea alongside the tree-lined road into the resort. Its beach is pebbly, but quite long and reasonably wide.

Srebreno, unlike Kupari, gives the impression of being rather more crowded, though the main hotel, the Orlando, has plenty of space. The pebbly beach, with sand under the stones, is fairly narrow, but very attractively backed by pines, tamarisks, cypresses, and other trees and shrubs. Because the beach shelves very gently it's ideal for children.

Mlini is an extraordinary, old-established, tiny village with a stream flowing through it, wild irises growing close to the water, and swans actually paddling around – which must be unique on the Yugoslav coast. The original Hotel Mlini, now modernised, fits very well into this rural scene. However, a vast new hotel, the Astarea, has now been built (a bit away from the village's centre), and an annexe of three-storey, village-like buildings added to the original hotel. The Hotel Mlini itself has expanded, too, but without changing its basic character. For years it has been extremely popular with British visitors, particularly the older folk who flock there throughout the winter.

These three resorts are barely 5 miles by road from Dubrovnik old town. There are regular bus services. Hotel launches operate to the Old Harbour in high season.

Plat

Kupari, Srebreno, and Mlini lie on broad Župa Bay's western side. **Plat**, in the bay's middle, pours itself down a long, pretty steep slope. There's a tiny old village astride the Magistrala on the slope's upper part. But you're hardly aware of it in the two hotels. The complex has been very ingeniously designed to fit the terrain, with restaurants, swimming pools, disco, and so on at different levels on your way down to the three fairly small pebbly beaches (you have to get up again too). The land around has been carefully landscaped. Pines and cypresses surround the hotels, and bare mountains loom above.

Cavtat and beyond

Cavtat was built centuries ago on the broader, higher, and longer prong of a two-pronged peninsula at Župa Bay's eastern end. It lies a mile or so off the Magistrala. Its very colourful, well-sheltered old harbour faces into the bay between the peninsula's two prongs. But there's another, smaller bay on the larger prong's further side. Cavtat's original small hotel, the Supetar (58 beds), stands on the waterfront. Five larger, very modern hotels, going up to almost 1000 beds in one case, are spread around the little town's two bays. All have pools and pebbly beaches close to them. You can hire boats from them all, and in some cases tennis and bowling are also available.

Cavtat's a pretty small place, and in July and August its visitor tally must be many times the permanent population's total. Yet it always seems peaceful. Maybe it's because of its remoteness (though the road to it is usually pretty crowded). Maybe it's the dense surrounding greenery.

76

Anyway, for generations it has been a place where people come to relax – including pre-war British royalty.

Edward VIII, in particular, used to sneak down here with Mrs Simpson and stay with the Račić family in their mansion high on the hill above the town. A mausoleum designed by the sculptor Meštrović (see Chapter 7), right on the hill's summit, commemorates Račić family members who died in the 'flu epidemic that followed WWI.

Cavtat's considered by many to have been the site of the Epidaurum from which Dubrovnik's original inhabitants came. It was originally settled by Greek colonists and taken over later by the Romans.

Back on the Magistrala you've not far to go before you reach Dubrovnik airport, close to the village of **Čilipi,** long famous for the Sunday folklore displays still put on by inhabitants in full traditional costume. The rich **Konavli** valley inland from the airport area has for centuries provided the region's vegetables and fruit.

In the Sutorina Hills a little beyond **Gruda** village you cross into the Republic of Montenegro.

Access and excursions

Dubrovnik airport serves the whole of this area. Reaching Klek–Neum or Orebić involves a 2½-hour coach journey. Though the actual distance is much less, it can take about the same time to get to the Elaphitic Islands because of the slower boat journey. An hour or so, at most, takes you to Dubrovnik and the resorts round it. Add a few minutes for Orašac and Slano.

Excursions include conducted tours of Dubrovnik (local youngsters serving as guides can be excellent), and all-day tours southward to Sveti Stefan and the Gulf of Kotor in Montenegro (Chapter 9) and northward up the Neretva valley to Čilipi and Mostar, briefly described in Chapter 7. Shorter trips are also organised to the Gučetić mansion's botanically rich parkland at Trsteno, to Mljet, the oyster beds at Ston, one or more of the Elaphitic Islands, Čilipi, and so on. These depend somewhat on which resort you choose. In some cases longer trips into inland Montenegro (Chapter 16) may also be organised. If excursions are important to you make careful enquiries in advance.

Chapter Nine

The Montenegrin Coast

The big change you notice when you finally leave Dalmatia is the absence of islands. For the 150-odd miles of road till you reach the Albanian frontier you can count on the fingers of one hand those that are more than just large rocks sticking out of the sea. For most of the way scrub-spattered mountains still drop steeply down to craggy coves. But they're no longer parallel with the coast. They clump about in all directions. That's a big change too. Their slopes are occasionally thickly wooded. Elsewhere they're bare. It's a mostly wild and forbidding coast.

Every now and again however you come to sheltered bays and beaches that have been turned into large and growing resorts. They've become extremely popular with modern summer sun-seekers. Most have beaches made of coarse sand mixed with a little shingle. The coast's final stretch is an enormous length of sand ending at the River Bojana. Albania begins on the river's further bank.

The Montenegrins call their country Crna Gora - Black Mountain. Monte Negro is the Italian translation.

The Gulf of Kotor

The first thing you come to driving south from Cavtat is one of this coast's most surprising features - the magnificent **Gulf of Kotor** (Boka Kotorska). This is a collection of four interlinked bays surrounded by tremendously high forbidding mountains that takes the sea a good 20 miles inland. The entrance bay leads into a larger one. Then a very narrow channel takes you into two more bays, arranged like petals on a stalk. Bare mountains rise above them to summits over 5000 feet high. Photographs of cruise ships in the Gulf's inmost section make you think it must be a Norwegian fjord – except for the all-too-characteristic church belltower that always seems to stand in the foreground.

You get your first staggering view of the Gulf from the Sutorina Hills as you cross the unnoticeable boundary into Montenegro. But it's only the outermost bay you're seeing.

A very popular resort stands close to its mouth – south-facing, well-sheltered **Hercegnovi**. Many new hotels have been built here above a string of mainly rocky–pebbly beaches. Some stand a little away from the town, best reached by boat. Most are grouped along the stretch of coast between Igalo, once a separate village about 1½ miles from the town centre, and Hercegnovi itself. The bay's well sheltered, so that pedalos, surfboards, kayaks, rowboats, and water-skiing are popular. Tennis courts and a bowling alley are also available. Hercegnovi's hillside setting of pines, palms, cypresses, flower gardens, and old houses is particularly charming. The atmosphere's one of tremendous warmth.

Hercegnovi has an extraordinary history of almost continuous war. It was attacked and occupied by almost everyone – Turks, Spaniards, Venetians, Austrians, French, Russians, then Austrians again until 1918, with the usual story of unrest between the wars and bitter war and civil war from 1941 to 1945. The town was founded in 1382 by the Bosnian King Tvrtko to give his country an outlet to the sea. The present border between Montenegro and Bosnia–Herzegovina runs about 10 miles inland.

Despite its background, Hercegnovi's a pleasant, peaceful, rambling spot today. You go into the old town through the main gate to its west. It has the town clock above it, built on the footings of a Turkish tower. St Hieronimus Church (with the prominent dome) stands on the foundations of a Turkish mosque. 400 years ago the great Turkish traveller Evliya Chelebi recorded that the town had 47 mosques and 3080 dwellings.

You can still see the Kanli Kula (Bloody Tower), once a Turkish prison, and the Venetian forts Citadela and Forte Mare, as well as remains of the Spaniards' Španjola fort on the hill above the town (it was largely destroyed by the 1979 earthquake, but is still a good viewpoint). In Savina, Hercegnovi's eastern suburb, there's a fascinating monastery with three churches and a splendid treasury. Also a Spanish church built in 1539.

About five miles from Hercegnovi you come into the Gulf's second bay, named after **Tivat**, a now largely industrial town on its further shore. And after 8 or 9 miles more you reach **Kamenari**, on the narrow channel leading to the Gulf's two inmost bays.

A very simple ferry takes you across to tiny Lepetane in a very few minutes if you're bent on a speedy journey southward or into inland Montenegro.

Lepetane's name's said to be a corruption of the Italian Le Putane – the Tarts. In sailing ship days the Gulf's sailors were well-known far and wide. It was here, they say, that the local ladies waited for them on their return from long months at sea.

If you keep going on the Gulf's Kamenari side a magnificent mountain vista opens up as you turn into Perast Bay. Soon after Kostanjica village a bridge takes the road over a 100-foot-high waterfall that's spectacular after recent rain – particularly since the water's pouring straight out of the rock, like the Ombla north of Dubrovnik (Chapter 8). Then you turn northeast along the bay's furthest side. All the time you're at the foot of steep lowering mountains.

Risan, tucked away in the bay's deepest corner, is the Gulf's oldest inhabited spot. It was the Illyrian Queen Teuta's capital in the 3rd century BC – hence the modern hotel's name – and managed to remain independent for a time when the Romans conquered the coast in 167 BC.

All sorts of archaeological remains have been discovered around Risan. Sir Arthur Evans worked here after discovering the vast Mycenean palace at Knossos on Crete. He unearthed remains of an ancient town's streets. There are prehistoric cliff drawings at nearby Lipci, "Cyclopean" walls made of gigantic stone blocks such as exist at many Mediterranean spots (eg, Pula – Chapter 4), a 2nd century AD Roman town mansion with excellent mosaic floors near the unsurfaced road leading inland over the mountains, and a lot else.

For today's visitors the medium-sized Hotel Teuta provides a comfortable stay with a staggering view from every room. Its design is very modern. It boasts an indoor swimming pool as well as a beach and a billiard table.

Your next stop, **Perast**, achieved its fame in more modern times. Its origins are ancient. But 400 years ago it became independent and its navy and shipyards flourished. Soon it founded its own naval academy, training ship's officers and producing the Adriatic's first navigation charts. When Peter the Great of Russia built Russia's first fleet for use in the Baltic (after he'd learned about shipbuilding in Amsterdam) he chose Matija Zmajević of Perast to command it.

The Russian naval flag presented to Zmajević by the Czar can still be seen in Perast's excellent little museum. It's housed in the Bujović family's Baroque mansion, built in 1693, at the height of Perast's prosperity. The Zmajević family mansion, built three years earlier, is also still standing, and so are several other fine Baroque homes. St Nicholas parish church's fascinating treasury includes the Order of Alexander Nevsky awarded to Admiral Zmajević by Peter the Great, a silver tablet depicting a 1654 battle in which little Perast defeated a Turkish force, and some fine church plate. The belltower which appears in all the pictures of cruise ships in the Gulf of Kotor belongs to an unfinished church next door to St Nicholas.

Everyone's fascinated by the two colourful little islands close to Perast. Both have churches on them. One, dedicated to St George (Sveti Juraj or Djordje or Đurađ), belonged to a 12th-century Benedictine monastery. The other, Our Lady of the Rocks (Gospa od Škrpjela), is said to have been built by a shipwrecked sailor who survived by clinging all night to a rock, and then persuaded his friends to construct a man-made island. The church contains fascinating paintings – one's enormous – and some 2000 silver votive tablets representing Perast ships. They were thank-offerings for safe return from the men who sailed them. Processions of garlanded boats make pilgrimages to the islands each 22 July and 15 August.

Beyond Perast you pass from Risan Bay into Kotor Bay. Some 5 miles on, near the village of Orahovac, you come to another waterfall pouring out of seemingly solid rock. After another 8 miles or so past semi-built-up flatland below the towering mountains you reach the Gulf's capital town. The main road bypasses the built-up approach area. But the views are still magnificent.

Kotor nestles below gaunt slopes, with linking fortifications climbing high up the mountain to preclude attack from above. It's a strange, unearthly-seeming place, full of twisting dark alleys and lovely little squares hidden behind vast Byzantine walls. Historically, it has been a battleground for Ilyrians, Romans, Slavs, Byzantines, Macedonians, Serbs, Hungarians, Dubrovnikans, Bosnians, Turks, French, Russians, and Austrians. From 1815 to 1918 it was a major Austro-Hungarian naval base. In 1918 Austria's "red sailors" mutinied here and their leaders were shot. In the 18th century, at the height of its independent maritime power, its Sailors' Fraternity, founded 900 years previously, covered 600 vessels.

Today the area's activity lies nearly all outside the walls. But the tiny medieval town's alleys and squares will

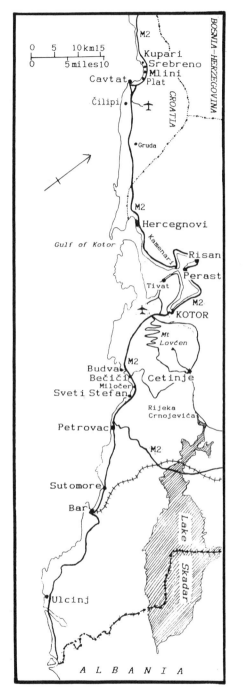

be well worth exploring once repairs of the 1979 earthquake damage are complete. You'll find a fascinating Romanesque cathedral dedicated to St Tryphon (Sveti Tripun), whose remains reached Kotor in 809. The church has been damaged several times. Its architecture's very mixed. It has a fine golden altarpiece however and a valuable collection of 18th-century church plate, the work of local craftsmen. It stands in the town square, along with a squat clocktower.

You can also see the Rector's Palace (Kotor's constitution was similar to Dubrovnik's and Venice's), a number of ornate patrician mansions, and several other churches dating back to 1195. Also the charming small Maritime Museum.

Repairs making good extensive damage from the 1979 earthquake have progressed well. Kotor has recently become yet another entry among UNESCO's 150 or so spots of world heritage importance.

You'll have passed the town's hotel, the Fjord, about half a mile before reaching the old town. It was built in 1986, and boasts a wonderfully peaceful position with superb views. There are places to swim nearby, and an indoor swimming pool.

Officially, the M2 Magistrala carries you right round the Gulf. But if you take the Kamenari–Letpetane ferry you cut across the hills and rejoin it on its way to Budva. Another road from Kotor takes you to Tivat and its airport.

The most amazing route out of Kotor however leads over the mountains to Montenegro's former capital, Cetinje, described below under Excursions. This is the famous Serpentin, still unsurfaced, that climbs in a series of

hairpin bends up what looks like a
vertical mountain wall. The road's little
used today. Coastal buses for Cetinje
go through Budva (see below), and
ordinary drivers take a steep but
newer and easier alternative road. If
you wander into the countryside
round Kotor you'll find astonishing old
paths, with steps cut in virgin rock at
their steepest points. Local people –
and their donkeys – used to go up and
down these at an amazing pace.

Budva and Bečiči

The miniature fortified peninsula town
of **Budva** was devastated by the 1979
earthquake. It's still closed to visitors
because of possible masonry falls. But
it's a fascinating spot. Settled since
prehistory, it appears to have started
its "modern" existence as a Greek
colony.

The oldest part of St John's church in
the town's centre is thought to be 7th
century, though its belltower was
added only in 1867. A Latin inscription
dates little St Mary-on-the-Point
church to AD 840. The other
churches, like most of the town's
walls, are a mere 400 or 500 years old.

Budva's minute harbour has become a
modern yacht marina. The hillside on
the town's further side is now largely
covered with extensions to the Hotel
Avala, which began its existence back
in 1936. You get from its self-catering
apartments to the main hotel by a lift.
Water-skiing and boat hire are
available, and there's a children's pool
and playground. The famous Mogren
beach that features in innumerable
brochure photographs – two sand-and-
pebble coves divided by a wood-
covered cliff – is about 300 yards
away. The much smaller Mogren
Hotel overlooks Budva's harbour.

A succession of large beaches begins

beyond Budva. Nearly all consist of
coarse sand with a mixture of small
pebbles, very suitable for children.
Because of this, many hotels make
special arrangements for their
youngest visitors.

Nowhere is this truer than at
Slovenska Plaža, just under a mile
east of Budva. It's a completely novel
type of self-contained holiday village
intended for all-age families. It includes
restaurants, shops, cafés, bars, two
swimming pools, lounges, tennis
courts, a bowling alley, basketball
ground, and even a chess centre.
Everything's linked by well-landscaped
avenues where the only traffic allowed
consists of small electric trucks. A
long public beach runs alongside. Here
Slovenska Plaža maintains two
children's play areas. Early suppers,
high chairs, cots, and so on are also
provided.

Some hotels at **Bečiči** also take extra
trouble with young guests. Bečiči was
originally just a vast beach of pebbles
mixed with sand of various colours,
with similar smaller beaches in nearby
coves. Since the early 1960s a number
of hotels have been built on flat land
directly inland. Some provide
children's pools and playgrounds,
early suppers, etc. Tennis, basket-ball,
volley-ball, and a pretty complete
range of watersports are also on offer.

Bečiči has proved very popular with
British guests. It stands on its own,
barely 2 miles from tiny Budva.

Miločer and Sveti Stefan

Miločer lies 3 miles south. It began as
a small royal summer residence, set in
lovely parkland above a delightful little
beach. It looks out seaward to the
island of Sveti Stefan (St Stephen),
described below. Miločer's original

building was turned into a very comfortable hotel in the 1960s, and more hotel accommodation, self-catering villas, shops, a swimming pool, etc have been added since then. The beaches at the foot of the hills here are mostly of coarse sand.

You can walk from Miločer to **Sveti Stefan**, most famous of all the area's hotels. When the war ended, the tiny island fishing settlement had been deserted by almost all its inhabitants, and the decision was taken to turn the entire stone-built village into a single luxury hotel. Work went slowly at first. But the result today is spectacular.

Sveti Stefan has been joined to the mainland by a causeway. But vehicles can't travel further than the entrance gate. The tiny roads and paths are much too narrow, their corners too sharp, and slopes far too steep. Instead of being accommodated in rooms you're given a cottage or part of one. The dining room gives you superb views along the coast. The cooking here is excellent.

Furnishings are mostly handmade in traditional local craft styles. The village's church and its little squares and lookout points have all been carefully preserved. You can swim from the island's private beach or in its pool, play tennis, read in its library, browse in its art gallery, and relax in its nightclub. Your seclusion and peace are complete.

A comfortable, but more ordinary hotel has ben built very close to the causeway's mainland end. It doesn't share Sveti Stefan's isolation. But it enjoys rather similar views of mountains and hills jostling the coast and little bays tucked between headlands thickly covered with pines, cypresses, oleanders, and scrub of various sorts. There's a sizeable beach of coarse sand directly below the hotel, as well as a pool. You look straight out towards Sveti Stefan.

Just to confuse you, Miločer, Sveti Stefan island, and the mainland hotel opposite the island are often treated as a single resort and all called Sveti Stefan or Miločer–Sveti Stefan. This seems a pity, because the three spots' characters and atmospheres are very different indeed.

Petrovac, Sutomore, and Bar

A few miles beyond Sveti Stefan the M2 turns inland. Another 8 or 9 miles of winding coastal road, clinging to the tumbling wooded hillslopes above the sea, bring you to a long bay of coarse sand. The once-tiny village of **Petrovac**, originally built at one end of the bay, today covers most of the land above the beach. A number of hotels have been built among the houses, on fairly flat land between the sea and the jumbled hills. Sub-tropical shrubs and flowers among pines, olives, oleanders, and cypresses add warmth to the scenery.

The fact that hotels and village are to some extent jumbled together on land that's not too heavily built up gives Petrovac a different feel from a lot of the resorts we've been considering. The tiny harbour's tucked under a headland at one end of the bay, which is bounded by rocky cliffs. A large new hotel has been built on a slope above a separate shingly beach just beyond the main bay. Windsurfing, bowling, boat hire, tennis, and billiards are available here. A footpath promenade takes you the mile into the village. There are several ancient churches and fortresses and the remains of a Roman "villa" nearby.

The M2 Magistrala turns inland at

Petrovac, to make for Titograd (Chapter 15), Kosovska Mitrovica and Peć (Chapter 13), and Skopje (Chapter 14), where it joins the M1 inland highway linking Ljubljana, Zagreb, and Belgrade with Gevgelija on the Greek frontier (Chapter 14) for Thessaloniki and Athens, with a branch at Niš (Chapter 13) going to Sofia, Bulgaria's capital, and Istanbul.

A good 15 miles along the winding road continuing along the coast brings you to **Sutomore**. It stands on yet another long bay, with a coarse sand beach a good mile long. Clumps of steep, rocky mountains bound the bay, with the tiny original village at its northern end. There has been less hotel building here. Two sizeable hotels have most of the beach to themselves. They stand in gardens at the foot of wooded mountain slopes.

After another 6 miles you come to **Bar**, which isn't a resort but a seaport whose activity's increasing every year. This includes regular car-and-passenger services to Bari in Italy, and to Corfu and Igoumenitsa in Greece, as well as Yugoslav coastal services. Its main link with the hinterland is the amazing railway line running all the way to Belgrade. Its route passes through regions still hardly served by roads. Building it involved boring innumerable long tunnels through the country's inland mountains. Work wasn't completed till the 1970s.

Bar lies a little off the Magistrala. Inland you'll see the jagged ruins of a town obviously destroyed by gunfire. Signposts leading to it say "Stari Bar" – Old Bar. In 1878, when the Montenegrins fought their way to the sea at Bar and Ulcinj (see below) the Turks retorted by obliterating the ancient settlement whose origins go back certainly to the 10th and possibly

the 6th century. Today it's preserved as an ancient monument under state protection. You can still see the remains of several old churches, the former bishop's palace, an aqueduct that brought water to the town, and much else.

Bar got its first road into the interior in 1888, and the first section of the railway that now runs all the way to Belgrade in 1908. In 1910 the Russian battleship Potemkin, later famous for the 1918 mutiny and the film made about it, anchored here, bringing the Czar's representative to the coronation of Montenegro's last king.

Ulcinj: the end of the road

Some 20 miles beyond Bar, **Ulcinj** seems an unlikely spot for a flourishing holiday resort. It's thought to have started its existence as an island village which sank during an earthquake. Romans and Byzantines ruled the later settlement. The Turks used it as a main base. 400 Algerians settled here to live by harassing Venetian shipping. Yugoslavia's only black citizens lived in Ulcinj, descendants of African slaves brought by the Algerians.

But a sandy beach almost 8 miles long stretches southward all the way to the River Bojana and the Albanian frontier. More and more hotels have been built beside it, and are still being built, mostly towards the south. The land inland is much flatter than the places we've been looking at, and there's plenty of room for gardens and trees. The beach is magnificent, and the spot's only small snag is that it's 50 miles by not very fast roads to Tivat airport, 64 to Dubrovnik, and 84 to Titograd. It's some consolation that you go through magnificent scenery from all three airports – provided the journey's done in daylight.

Tennis, surfboarding, water skiing, bowls, and boat and cycle hire are all available. Basket-ball, volley-ball, and hand-ball, too, at some hotels. The beach is really ideal for children, and some hotels cater specially for them.

Access and excursions

Flights serving Montenegro's coastal resorts may arrive at Dubrovnik, Tivat, or Titograd airports and, as we've said, the journey to those furthest south can be a bit long. If this worries you, get detailed information via your travel agent.

Excursions vary a lot. Outings to Dubrovnik by boat or coach are popular. So are trips exploring the Gulf of Kotor, described above. You can travel inland to **Cetinje**, Montenegro's wonderfully-located former capital. It lies in a typical karst-country "polje", a fertile bowl surrounded by bare limestone mountains.

Cetinje was used as Montenegro's base for its centuries-long struggle for independence from the Turks (Chapter 16). It's a colourful, but not specially spectacular town. Everything, including the royal palace, is pretty modest in size. But it's fascinating to see the monastery which housed Montenegro's first printing press (in the 16th century, after it had been moved from Obod fortress), the foreign embassies and legations established after 1878, when the whole world expressed its admiration for the Montenegrins' determination in driving the invaders out, the little hospital built in 1873, and the streets of colourful tiny old houses where ordinary people still live. A series of small museums recounts the Republic's and the town's history.

There's a problem however about enjoying them without a guide. Virtually all public notices in Cetinje (and in Montenegro generally, away from areas frequented by large numbers of foreign tourists) use the Cyrillic script (see Chapter 19). If you're not familiar with it, merely deciphering names can be a problem.

An outing to Cetinje may also give you the chance to see the **Njegoš mausoleum** where Montenegro's greatest prince–bishop ruler, Petar II Petrović Njegoš (Njegoš for short) is buried. He not only fought the Turks ferociously. He was also an exceptionally good and popular ruler. And as a poet he is still world-famous.

When only 32 he built a chapel to be his tomb nearly 6000 feet up on one of Mount Lovćen's summits. He died only six years later, but through fear of Turkish attacks his body wasn't taken to Mount Lovćen for several years. Then, when the Austrians occupied Montenegro during World War I, his remains were moved back to Cetinje. He wasn't reburied on Mount Lovćen till 1925. Respect and affection for him never died however. A new and very imposing mausoleum commissioned from the sculptor Ivan Meštrović was finally completed in 1974. Inside it there's a seated figure of Njegoš, over 12 feet high and weighing 28 tons.

You reach the tomb from the car park through a 275-foot tunnel that rises nearly 300 feet with the aid of 441 steps. The view from the top takes in the Gulf of Kotor and many of Montenegro's mountain peaks. It's worth the climb. The area has been made one of Yugoslavia's two "historic" National Parks.

Trips into Montenegro may show you also the Republic's modern capital,

Titograd (Chapter 16). It was founded on an ancient site, but its buildings consist mostly of vast flats, factories, and offices.

On the way to Titograd, if your driver takes the old road you pass the waterlily-covered shallow fringes of **Lake Skadar** (Skadarsko Jezero), where the Crnojević rulers set up sanctuary. A third of the lake belongs to Albania. You may also see the enchanting little village called **Rijeka Crnojevića** (Crnojević River) at the lake's northern extremity. It's a green and fertile 19th-century settlement, built on a tangle of canal-like river branches in the middle of olives, orchards, vines, and pinewoods. Originally it was just a stores base below the hilltop fortress, Obod, where the Crnojević rulers set up their HQ in 1475, between being driven by the Turks from their lake-island capital, Žabljak (not the Žabljak mentioned below) and settling in Cetinje.

Other outings show you the spectacular **Morača** and/or **Tara Gorges** northeast of Titograd. They're among the world's deepest. They're described in Chapter 16.

A very full day's extension of the Morača Gorge excursion takes you to **Žabljak** on the slopes of Mount Durmitor right in the heart of Montenegro's mountains. It gives you a glimpse of the Durmitor National Park, listed by UNESCO as a natural heritage site of world importance. The Park's described briefly in Chapter 16.

Shorter trips show you the **Reževići** and **Paraskevica Monasteries** close to Budva, and take you by boat along the coast, or by coach to the Albanian frontier at **Hani i Hottit** on Lake Skadar. The Albanians, hard up for Western currencies and not geared to cope with masses of Western sightseers, unfortunately don't permit day visits by tourists not paying (in Western currency) for at least one night's accommodation. You have to come back to Britain and book another holiday.

INLAND YUGOSLAVIA

Chapter Ten

Slovenia and the Yugoslav Alps

We've spent most of this book describing the coast. Yet we've done little more than outline its appeal. And the coast anyway is a very specialised and limited part of Yugoslavia. At least as much space could be given to half-a-dozen or more of the country's other aspects and areas. Till recently these have been the preserve either of specialists (such as the rare historians of Byzantine art, architects, or wildlife specialists) or of dedicated travellers prepared to brave the problems produced by lack of surfaced roads, scarcity of any hotels (let alone modern ones), and the difficulties of getting information and help when you don't speak the local language.

Things are changing fast however. The coast's beginning to be recognised for its superb yachting. Magnificent inland regions that non-Yugoslavs had never heard of 10 years ago are now covered by packaged walking and wildlife holidays. Coach tours visit fine towns and outstanding National Parks. Yugoslavia's superb medieval monasteries and other astonishing art remains, its wonderful fishing, and excellent lake and river canoeing, as well as more superb National Parks and breathtaking scenery still remain to be "discovered". But it won't be long before Yugoslavia's one of Europe's major holiday regions.

Slovenia's Alpine mountain resorts

Even before WWI many of Slovenia's mountain spots were well-known to the relatively few Austrians, Hungarians and others who could afford holidays. They're really coming into their own today. Slovenia's the small Republic tucked into Yugoslavia's northwestern corner. Its area includes outliers of Europe's central Alpine range, the so-called Julian, Krawanken, and Kamnik Alps. The best-known holiday spots are grouped around the mighty **Triglav** mountain. The highest of its three peaks tops 9000 feet and is included in the impressive Triglav National Park.

Bled, directly east and itself 1600 feet above sea level, is the queen of the region's summer resorts and nowadays popular too with ski beginners and intermediates. Its setting could hardly be more fairylike, with a castle clinging to a high rocky outcrop beside the town, a colourful church perched on a tiny deserted island in the middle of its large, placid lake (Blejsko Jezero or Lake Bled), and its heavily wooded valley ringed by magnificent mountain peaks. Only rowboats and yachts are allowed, so your peace is never disturbed by powerboats' strident screams.

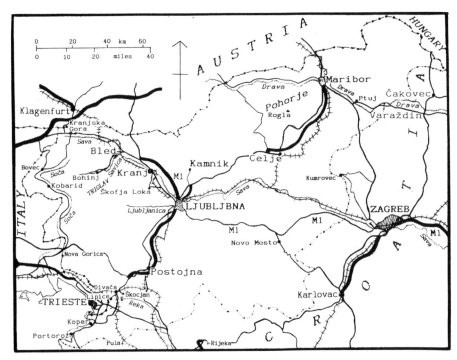

Hotels and self-catering accommodation are scattered round one end of the lake, at varying distances from what was once a tiny village. In summer you've a huge range of walks on well-marked paths, boat trips on the lake, swimming (temperatures often reach 80°F), and excursions to nearby spots in Yugoslavia, Italy, and Austria. Tennis, bowls, horse-riding, and cycle and boat hire are available. Bled also boasts Yugoslavia's only golf course (May to October only).

In winter a free ski bus takes you 5 miles south to the main ski area, with chair and drag lifts serving other stretches – 10 miles of runs in all. Buses serve other ski spots if you want. The lake normally freezes, so that you can skate on it or walk across.

Bohinj lies higher up the same valley, beside a larger lake, with a splendid waterfall above it. In summer Bohinj's full of families who obviously take their walking seriously. The heart of the superb Triglav National Park, with its soaring peaks, mountain lakes, and Alpine flowers, can be reached on foot. In winter free buses take you to ski areas with 15 miles of marked runs and even longer cross-country pistes. As in Bled, bars and restaurants are very reasonable. Après-ski entertainment's relatively modest.

The region's main ski resort is **Kranjska Gora**, north of the Triglav on the main road leading from Slovenia's capital, Ljubljana (Laibach in German), to Tarvisio in Italy. Immediately north of the town the easy Wurzen Pass (Koren sedlo to Yugoslavs) takes you into Austria. There are ski areas on both sides of Kranjska Gora, and some hotels stand right beside nursery slopes. Beginners and intermediates are specially well catered for, but World Cup pistes attract experts too. Here your evenings can be as quiet or as lively as you like. Discos keep going till the early hours. And in summer the town becomes an excellent place for relaxation and mountain walks as strenuous or gentle as you wish.

Gozd, or **Gozd Martuljek** to distinguish it from other Gozds, is a tiny village 2 miles east of Kranjska Gora. It lies in a typical Alpine valley with a magnificent mountain backdrop. Paths indicated by coloured markers in the normal Alpine fashion give you a tremendous choice of walks. A cable car takes you high into the mountains. Spring flowers make the hillsides specially attractive.

West of the Triglav, some 27 miles south of Kranjska Gora, **Bovec** on the River Soča is emerging as a modern mountain holiday spot. Its hotels are mostly fairly modest, but the scenery's superb. Tennis, bowling, bicycle hire, and fishing are all possible.

Who ever heard of little **Kobarid**, 13 miles south of Bovec? The answer is – the whole world, but under its Italian name Caporetto. It's where one of WWI's decisive battles was fought on the frontier between Italy and what was then Austria, and it's where Hemingway's great novel, Farewell to Arms, begins. The friendly little Hotel Matajur can point out the best walks, provide you with a fishing licence, and arrange for you to use all the sporting facilities of the local high school. The Soča gorge near Kobarid is impressive.

These aren't Slovenia's only Alpine resorts. There are scores of other delightful spots, including **Krvavec** in the high Kamnik Alps north of Ljubljana, barely 15 miles from the capital's airport, and the nearby town of **Kamnik**, itself now a package tour destination.

Ljubljana and other towns

Slovenia's capital **Ljubljana** contains a remarkable mass of fine buildings. They range from early Baroque, notably the Civic Square below the medieval hilltop castle in the old town's heart, to some splendid modern shops, offices, and flats and the new (1959) Republic Assembly Building, Slovenia's Parliament. Art nouveau is represented in some turn-of-the-century architecture (eg, Pogačnik House in Cigale Street, 1901). Art deco appears in the Cooperative Credit Bank (1922), the University Library (1938), and elsewhere. The old houses beside the River Ljubljanica close to the Triple Bridge (1931) make a particularly attractive scene.

Careful town planning on original lines was a feature of Ljubljana's 19th-century development. The town was seen as a series of settlements linked by parks. The railway's arrival, and then the 1895 earthquake upset plans somewhat. But the tradition of thoughtful planning was never lost – not even during WWII and its ghastly aftermath. The city's National Museum, its National Gallery, Gallery of Modern Art, cathedral of St Nicholas, and National Theatre are all worth seeing.

But Ljubljana isn't Slovenia's only fine town. **Maribor**, 11 miles from the Austrian border on the road from Ljubljana to Graz in Austria, has a magnificent late medieval centre facing the River Drava, as well as highly industrialised modern suburbs and mountain resorts, such as **Rogla**, in the nearby Pohorje heights. Tiny **Ptuj**, 17 miles southeast, is a gem of a town, built on a low hill also beside the Drava. Its old town hall, town square, town tower, and arcaded courtyard of the castle crowning the hill are all delightful. So are some of its modern areas.

Little **Celje**, halfway between Ljubljana and Maribor, is famous for its medieval appearance. **Novo Mesto**, halfway between Ljubljana and Zagreb, capital of neighbouring Croatia (Chapter 11), **Kranj**, between Ljubljana and Bled, and **Škofja Loka**, 6 miles south of Kranj, are all worth visits. All lie in fertile, rolling hill country. All show clear links with the sort of decorated buildings you find in Austria, Southern Germany, Switzerland, and Italy's South Tyrol. All are charming. They all provide also hotels and private-house accommodation. There are lots of pleasant spas, too, in Slovenia's hills.

Some other attractions

We've mentioned in Chapter 4 the Postojna and Škocjan Caves and the Lipice stud farm close to the frontier at Trieste. It remains to add only that Europe's E6 international long-distance footpath runs right across Slovenia, from the Alpine Eibiswald-Ivnik Austrian frontier post to Matjuli above Opatija in Croatia (see Chapter 4), and that many Slovenian farms offer visitors accommodation and meals. The farm families may not speak English. But many still speak good German.

Chapter Eleven

Inland Croatia

Croatia's heart lies in its splendid capital, Zagreb. And Zagreb lies in the heart of this oddly-shaped Republic. Its northern section is called Zagorje (Over-the-Hill – beyond the hills north of Zagreb, that is). East of that lies Slavonia, part of the great Pannonian Plain, bounded by the Hungarian frontier, the Danube, and the Sava. Well to the west lies Istria (Chapter 4). The portion immediately south and southwest of Zagreb comprises the wooded Gorski Kotar hills, the Kapela mountains with the Plitvice National Park on their edge, and the Lika valley between Kapela and Velebit (Chapter 5). A long tail that becomes continuously narrower (from 40 miles in the north to 5 or less and eventually nil near Dubrovnik) takes in all Dalmatia's coastland apart from Bosnia–Herzegovina's largely symbolic corridor to the sea at Neum (Chapter 8).

It's difficult not to treat Istria, the "Croatian Littoral" (Chapter 5), and Dalmatia and all the offshore islands north of Montenegro as separate from the Republic's main inland bulk. That's what we've already done. Istria and Dalmatia differ from each other. But inland Croatia differs even more from both.

Historically, Croatia was dominated by Rome till the 6th-7th-century invasions by Goths, and Slav and other tribes. Then Hungary, the Turks, and later Austria–Hungary became its rulers, with incursions from Tatars and Turks at varying dates. In 1918 it was made part of the Kingdom of Yugoslavia. But a nationalist political faction kept up violent opposition to the Serbs and almost everyone else.

The Croats call their country Hrvatska (the H sounds almost like a K: see Chapter 19) and themselves Hrvatski. They're the reason why men wear ties today. Some 300 years ago European aristocrats and gentry were much taken with the white neckcloths worn by Croatian mercenaries. Sporting "cravats" (kravatski) became the fashion. Before long the new accessories were known colloquially as "ties". It's all in the big Oxford English Dictionary (the 25-volume version).

Zagreb

Because **Zagreb** seemed so out of reach in the early postwar years, even when tourism was beginning to flourish gently on the coast, people have often imagined it's some sort of backward, undeveloped, or at least under-developed, city. The reverse in fact is true. Apart from postwar doldrums – inevitable given the incredible destruction Yugoslavia suffered (Chapter 17) – Zagreb has for centuries been in the forefront of commerce, industry, science, and the arts.

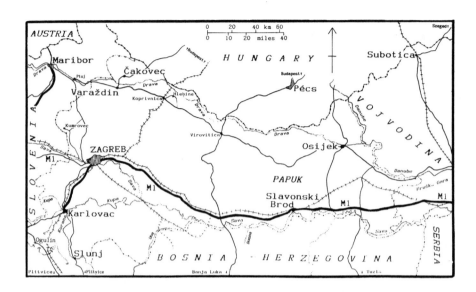

Its Trade Fair is the world's third oldest. The Yugoslav Academy of Arts and Sciences has its seat in Zagreb. The city's University has been prominent for well over a century. The Ethnographic Museum's a model for museums of its type. Any city would be proud of its superb, spaciously sited Croatian National Theatre, with one of Meštrović's best-loved sculptures, the Source of Life, in front of it. Any city would be proud, too, of the vast new Vatroslav Lisinski concert hall.

Strossmayer's Gallery of Old Masters contains Yugoslavia's largest collection of 14th–19th-century West European painting. In Ivan Meštrović's Studio (where he worked) you can see part of his output. And the Primitive Art Gallery contains not only the country's largest collection of Yugoslavia's outstanding naive painters' works (see Hlebine, below), it also offers a constantly-changing selection for sale at very reasonable prices.

The city consists of two main parts. The oldest is Gornji Grad (Upper Town), itself split into higher and lower areas. The higher's still largely medieval and reached more speedily by stepped lanes than by car. Under the name Gradec (Grič in Zagreb dialect) it got its first charter from King Béla IV of Hungary in 1242. Its little St Mark's church, noted for its coloured rooftiles, dates from the 14th century. The bishop, based in his cathedral on flat land east of Gradec in an area still called Kaptol (Chapter House, also the name of a main street), tried to dominate the Upper Town. Bloody battles resulted. The two nuclei were combined only in 1850.

Forty years later a fine new area, the Donji Grad (Lower Town) began to be laid out grid-pattern-wise to the south, with lots of spacious green squares and fine buildings. This is now divided between fine older areas and new parts that are still spreading southwards. Much new building's excellent. The sprawling east–west suburbs are less attractive. A century ago the city also began edging northward into the Zagrebačka Gora hills. This is the really smart place to live. Out here, too, you'll find the town's vast, superb municipal cemetery, a very well-kept open-air art gallery in itself.

Zagreb can be hot and stuffy in summer, and cold in winter. It boasts some excellent hotels, which inevitably aren't cheap. Its restaurants are also good – and not expensive.

The Zagorje

Varaždin, almost due north of Zagreb, is the Zagorje's main city. It's an industrial base today, but grew up as a fortified town around a 13th-century castle. The old town's centre has been charmingly pedestrianised.

The Zrinski family responsible for Varaždin castle built an even larger fortress at **Čakovec**, 10 miles north on the road to the Hungarian border and Budapest. It guarded the flat, marshy Međimurje area between the Rivers Mura and Drava, now famous mostly for its hunting, Čakovec's pedestrianised old centre is attractive.

Hlebine, roughly 40 miles east of Varaždin, was where Yugoslav naive painting began around 1930. The artist Krsto Hegedusić started encouraging local people to paint, using the old tradition of tempera on glass. Their brilliantly inimitable (but much imitated) work soon became famous worldwide. The third generation of peasant painters is now producing masterpieces. There's a gallery of their work at Hlebine.

The place that thousands of visitors flock to is tiny **Kumrovec**, about 25 miles northwest of Zagreb. It's here that Josip Broz, better known as Marshal Tito, the Yugoslav's outstanding wartime leader and peacetime statesman, was born in 1896. His birthplace is now a museum.

The Zagorje region's rolling hills and busy farms and villages make it extremely attractive just to wander through.

Gorski Kotar, Kapela, and the Lika Valley

Much the same can be said of the area south and southwest of Zagreb – except that the hills are very much higher, and snow-capped up to six months a year. **Delnice**, barely 25 miles from Rijeka on the road from Zagreb, used to be a popular ski centre. But its equipment hardly satisfies modern skiers, and an important brand new resort is taking shape at **Ogulin**. Unable to raise Western-style capital, development seems to hang on shoestrings. Yet progress is accelerating, and runs on the north-facing slopes of Bjelolasica, the Kapela range's highest peak, will undoubtedly soon be attracting international attention. Snow's plentiful here for six months each year. Ogulin has already put in a bid for the 1992 Winter Olympics. There's an impressive swallow-hole, incidentally, with a sizeable river disappearing into it, in the town centre. Two other nearby rivers emerge fully-formed from hillsides. After flowing normally for a few miles they too disappear into the ground.

The artificial **Lokve Youth Lake** (Omladinsko Jezero) in the Gorski

Kotar, about 20 miles from Rijeka (Chapter 5) and 5 from Delnice, is now a base for UK-packaged holidays. It's part of an inland mountain resort in the Rišnjak National Park whose altitudes range from 3500 to 5500 feet above sea level. Rare Alpine edelweiss grows here and the park has the mixed vegetation of Mediterranean and continental climates.

Karlovac, 28 miles southwest of Zagreb at the end of a motorway stretch that will one day be continued to Rijeka past this fine National park, is a large, messy town and best avoided. **Slunj**, 35 miles south, on the other hand, is distinctly attractive. It's dominated by a picturesque 13th-century castle that did a lot to delay the Turks' northward advance to the gates of Vienna. **Plitvice National Park**, which we looked at briefly in Chapter 5, lies some 20 miles south of Slunj. The **Lika valley**, between Plitvice's hills and the Velebit (see Chapter 5) has nothing of special interest, except that it's a rich farming area. Gospić is its main town.

Slavonia

Most tourists aren't likely to spend much time in Slavonia – even though it's Croatia's most heavily-populated region, and certainly its most fertile. Lying between Danube and Sava, with the Drava flowing through its northern part, it's the beginning of the great Pannonian Plain that takes in the whole Vojvodina (Chapter 11) and extends into Hungary's Great Plain. Its main town is industrial **Osijek**.

Apart from 2000-foot-high **Mount Papuk**, Slavonia's largely flat. Almost the only town much noticed by foreigners – and then only by railway addicts – is southern **Slavonski Brod**. Halfway between Zagreb and Belgrade on the Simplon–Orient route to Athens and Istanbul, the great international expresses stop there. But why the strange name? Simple. Slavonski Brod means "Slavonian Boat" (or ferry), and it's matched by Bosanski Brod (Bosnian Boat) on the broad Sava's southern bank. The Sava forms the boundary here between Croatia and Bosnia-Herzegovina (Chapter 16).

Chapter Twelve

Northern Serbia and the Vojvodina

Serbia's the largest of Yugoslavia's constituent Republics. It contains an astonishing range of scenery – high mountains, spectacular mountain gorges, rolling green hillsides, vast, flat plain, great rivers, remote valleys, and fine towns. And scattered among all this you'll find impressive traces of all the peoples who've inhabited the land.

One prehistoric Danube site has thrown up unexpected evidence of surprisingly advanced artistic ability and social organisation from 8000–4500 BC. Wandering Celtic tribes who penetrated all Europe in the 3rd century BC left clear evidence of their lengthy stay. Traces of the Romans who conquered them and ruled the country for some 400 years can be seen at several spectacular archaeological sites. The Byzantines who took the region over when the Roman Empire split in two left fortresses and other traces.

The Slavs who drove them out were themselves soon converted to Christianity by Byzantine missionaries and soon began building monasteries whose churches are still decorated with astonishingly lovely and lively frescos. The Turkish invasion shut these superb lovely buildings with their superb paintings away from Western eyes. They began to be discovered barely a century ago. Turkish occupation in fact closed off nearly all the Eastern Church's wonderful art and architecture. It began to be studied effectively only in the 1920s, and is still very little known, even to art historians.

Belgrade

Serbia's and Yugoslavia's capital is **Belgrade** (Beograd to Yugoslavs). It's not a city you fall in love with at first sight. You see few fine buildings as you arrive. The place looks dusty and untidy. And well it may! It's Europe's most fought-over capital. On just one day in 1941 25,000 of its citizens were killed, several times that many injured, and a huge number of its buildings demolished in a single air raid. That was only one of WWII's devastating air raids. And even they make up only a fraction of the many occasions on which Belgrade has been attacked and mostly destroyed in its long existence.

One of its main problems today is that so many of the houses in the old town are too old and decrepit for modern standards, and too many of its roads, drains and water-supply conduits falling apart. Many side-roads still aren't properly surfaced. None were when war broke out in 1939. Yet despite new suburbs Belgrade people love their old city. You will too, once you get to know it.

When Belgrade folk want a cheery night out they flock to the bohemian restaurants and bars of the quarter called Skadarlija. It's based on Skadarska ulica (Skadar Street), close

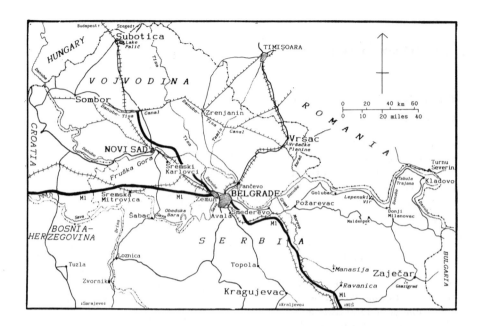

to Trg Republike (Republic Square). Here you can eat, drink, meet your friends, sing, play the fool as much as you like, argue, enjoy the music that others provide, and have a great deal of gentle fun till the early hours.

Republic Square and Marx and Engels Square (Trg Marksa i Engelsa), linked by the busy, wide street called Terazije, lined with shops, offices, and restaurants, are joint centres of the town that grew up in recent centuries south and east of high Kalemegdan hill, Belgrade's original nucleus. Kalemegdan commands the strategically vital point where the mighty Sava and even vaster Danube meet. Views from the top are superb. The park laid out around the ancient remains is charming. It's a cool, airy spot on hot summer days.

Most of the sightseeing you'll want to do starts close to Republic Square. The National Museum, which displays all manner of treasures from Lepenski Vir carvings (below) to Mycenean gold masks found at Trebeniŝte near Ohrid (Chapter 14), the famous Dupljaja votive chariot dating from about 1500 BC, and a contemporary model of the statue of Athena by Phidias, erected on Athens' Acropolis almost 2500 years ago, down to works by European painters such as Matisse, Picasso, and Chagall, stands actually in the square. It faces the National Theatre.

A short walk away, in Studentski Trg (Students' Square), you'll find the Ethnographic Museum, with items covering every part of Yugoslavia. You can also see the original University building and remains of a Roman public bath in the square too. The Frescos Gallery, containing exact copies of all the important frescos from the country's astounding medieval monasteries is close by. And round the corner you'll find the only surviving mosque from the scores the city once possessed. The Serbian Orthodox Church Museum stands close to Kalmegdan Park's main entrance.

The town's main shops and many of its best restaurants lie close to these two squares. Wide avenues spread south and east from them. In these you can see the fine Federal Parliament building (at Marx and Engels Square's further end), and the Serbian Parliament in Bulevar Maršala Tita (Marshal Tito Avenue), leading off the square.

Pioneers' Park (Pionirski Park), dedicated to children and full of entertainments designed for them, stands right in front of the Yugoslav Parliament. Some way past it, in Bulevar Revolucije (Revolution Avenue), you'll find the popular sports centre called Tašmajdan. Its Olympic-sized swimming pool gets pretty full on hot summer days.

On the Drava's west bank a whole new town, Novi Beograd (New Belgrade), links the 19th-century city to the separate town of Zemun. Its vast concrete structures look impressive, but not very attractive. Two very modern buildings that everyone does admire, the Sava Centre and the Gallery of Modern Art, stand on the Sava's left bank, close to the old town. Tito's Belgrade residence and his white marble tomb are also open to visitors.

If you arrive in Belgrade by bus or train, you'll find yourself close to the Sava's right bank and the quays where the Danube passenger boats serving West German, Austrian, Czechoslovakian, Hungarian, Yugoslav, Romanian, and Bulgarian river ports berth. The airport bus

deposits you close to the city's centre. Hotels are scattered through most of the central area and Novi Beograd. You can book private-house accommodation at very reasonable prices from the Tourist Office near the bus and railway stations.

The Vojvodina

The plain you see from Kalemegdan on the Danube's further side is part of the Vojvodina. This is a self-governing Autonomous Province that was previously part of Serbia. It's linked to Hungary's Great Plain and to Slavonia (Chapter 11). Three distinct regions make up the territory – the Banat (once ruled by a Turkish Ban), stretching from the Romanian frontier to the River Tisa, the Bačka (which takes its name from a now-ruined town) between Tisa and Danube, and Srem between Danube and Sava.

Bačka's flat. So is the Banat apart from the Vršac hills (Vršačke planine). Both are criss-crossed by rivers and vast canals which provide nearly 1000 miles of good canoeing that no one's aware of outside Yugoslavia (except a few Hungarians). There are fine sandy beaches beside the Tisa. Srem includes the Fruška Gora hills. The Vojvodina's boundary circles north of Belgrade, sometimes only a few miles away.

This is a prosperous region. It's also Europe's most ethnically mixed area. Its radio has to broadcast in five main languages – Serbian, Hungarian, Romanian, Slovak, and Ukrainian. But German, Czech, and other languages are also spoken, and a babel of tongues is used in newspapers, books, theatres, and films. Some nationalities lived here long before the days when manufacturing-based economy first demanded closed frontiers to protect sales. Others were deliberately encouraged by successive foreign rulers to settle for political reasons.

Novi Sad

The Vojvodina's capital, **Novi Sad**, lies beside the Danube, with the Srem region's Fruška Gora hills ending opposite it. The city's old centre has been very attractively pedestrianised. Narrow streets alternate with open squares, filled with shops, cheerful restaurants, and churches. Part of the Vojvodina Museum's excellent collection includes a magnificent gilt helmet, once part of a Roman general's dress uniform.

You'll find a very attractive park on open ground beside the Danube. From here you look across the broad river to **Petrovaradin** fortress. Once it guarded a pontoon bridge's southern end, and played an important part in Hungary's and later Austria's battles against the Turks. It's got 10 miles of underground galleries hidden in its hill. Today it houses the Novi Sad Town Museum, artists' and craftsmen's studios, and the Varadin Hotel.

Banat, Bačka, and Srem

Vršac in the Banat, on the road to Timişoara in Romania, has a semi-Romanian character. There are a lot of 18th-century buildings in its centre. They include the Bishops's Palace, a little-changed apothecary's, and a galleried inn called the Two Pistols. Karadjordje, leader of Serbia's 1804 rising against the Turks, once stayed here. Strapped for cash, he left two pistols in lieu of payment. Forests, orchards, vineyards, and streams and springs abound in the Vršac hills south of the town. Their highest point's altitude is some 2000 feet. Still

further south the **Deliblato Sands** (Deliblatska Peščara), once Europe's only sand desert, has been turned into a huge forested area.

Subotica, in the Bačka, contrasts with Vršac by being semi-Hungarian. It once belonged to the feudal lord the Hungarians revere as a national hero under the name Janos Hunyadi. Since he also owned estates in Romania the Romanians are equally proud of him, but know him as Iancu of Hunedoara. Subotica boasts a Roman Catholic cathedral, an Orthodox church, and a Jewish synagogue, as well as a highly decorated Town Hall, built in 1910, and a fascinating town museum.

The once-derelict area to the town's southeast now consists of vineyards, orchards, and acacia groves, with reclaimed **Lake Palić** extensively used for watersports.

Sombor, in the Bačka, also has links with nearby Hungary. It's the Srem region however that offers most to foreign visitors. **Sremska Mitrovica** contains fine 18th- and 19th-century buildings. Its main importance, though, is its excavations. Sirmium, one of the late Roman Empire's four capitals, lies under it. A fair part of the Roman city has been uncovered, including what was almost certainly the imperial palace. You can see much of the excavations and a lot of lovely things from Srem in the town's Srem Museum. The Srem region gets its name of course from Roman Sirmium.

While Roman remains are rich and frequent in Srem, nothing equivalent has been found beyond the Danube in the Banat or Bačka. People who've never seen the river (including lots who should know better) write glibly that since time immemorial it has been a major trade route, and a help to movement, and so on. This is nonsense. Left to itself, as it was till about 150 years ago, the vast river's almost impossible to use. Before the modern dykes were built it used to flood twice a year to a width of 20 miles or more. Even finding your way among innumerable islands was almost impossible in a sailboat. Navigation from point to point began only with the invention of steamships, the buoying of main channels, and the building of the dykes.

Till this century only one bridge was ever built – in AD 105 by the Roman Emperor Trajan (see below) – across the Danube's 1000 miles below Budapest. It took the Romans very few years to realise that the Danube made a far more easily defended frontier than any walls in the style of the "limes" which surrounded the whole of their empire (eg, Hadrian's Wall in Northern England). They very quickly abandoned the areas they conquered in Romania (below).

Sremski Karlovci, some 6 miles southeast of Novi Sad, is renowned as the region's most beautiful town. Though ancient in origin, most of what you see today dates from the last 200 years. There's an old courthouse, an 1890 apothecary's, the former Serbian Orthodox Patriarchate built in 1894, an Orthodox cathedral from 1762 and a Catholic church from 1768, a grammar school from 1891, and much else.

The **Obedska Bara** Nature Reserve in Srem's remotest southern region, beside a large oxbow lake left from an earlier Sava meander, is one of Europe's most important bird migration centres.

It's the old monasteries tucked away in the more northerly **Fruška Gora** hills (now a National Park), however, that attract most visitors. They lie in

little valleys which, even today, need a lot of finding. Many were established by refugee monks from southern Serbia in the first centuries of Turkish rule. Most were built in semi-fortified style, with the church behind a quadrangle of buildings. Several contain notable frescos. The best-known include **Jazak**, **Krušedol**, **Grgeteg**, and **Hopovo Novi**. Krušedol's considered a treasure-house of 16th–18th-century Serbian painting. Its walls were covered twice over, once in fresco and once in oils, with moving compositions. Hopovo Novo's early 17th-century artist, the monk Mitrofan, specialised in vivid and realistic narrative scenes. His work, covered with whitewash, was discovered only after WWII.

The road along the Fruška Gora's crest which makes finding these monasteries so much easier was constructed by Partisans during WWII (Chapter 17).

The Danube lands east of Belgrade

In eastern Serbia the Danube scenery grows increasingly wild. Your first shock however is the jagged ruins of the vast **Smederevo** fortress, right beside the sea-like Danube, 30 miles from Belgrade. The ruins rise from the still flat land like some outsize set for a horror movie.

They were designed to guard the junction of the route eastward along the Danube's southern bank and the Great Morava valley route leading south to Sofia and Istanbul and to Thessaloniki and Greece.

Smederevo was once Serbia's capital. Its ruler had his palace inside the walls. Dubrovnik traders settled in the town outside its walls (Chapter 8). The Turks' capture of Smederevo in 1459 marked the end of medieval Serbia. The fortress changed hands repeatedly between Austrians and Turks for centuries, and was finally handed back to Serbia in 1867.

The Royal Navy's Danube Handbook of 1919 reports that there were 19,000 dwellings then inside the fortifications (it's the only serious guide to the river ever written, commissioned when it was first made an international waterway and still useful). The buildings vanished in a 1941 gunpowder explosion and fire that also removed 5000 inhabitants. Children play peacefully and lovers wander inside the forbidding walls today, while enthusiasts fish from the river bank. The Danube supplies an amazing variety of fish, including caviar-providing sturgeon in the delta which Romania shares with the USSR.

Beyond Smederevo, marshes force the main road to abandon the river bank. You go through **Požarevac**, centre of rich farmland, which holds the spectacular Ljubičevo International Equestrian Games early every autumn. Then you turn northeast again and about 33 miles on reach the river at one of its most spectacular points.

It's the start of what was once the **Iron Gate** gorge, the "Djerdap" to Yugoslavs. The huge river's forced into a channel which, even today, may be little more than 80 yards wide. Once it was turbulent and dangerous. The most powerful tugs managed barely 2–3 knots against the stream. Today, the river level has risen a good 60 feet thanks to the vast dam at Kladovo, beyond the gorge's further end. It provides both Romania and Yugoslavia with electricity, and has turned the once-boiling gorge – still called Kazan (the Cauldron) – into a peaceful pleasure lake and easy navigation route.

At **Golubac** the road starts running close to the river. But it's high on mountains above it, with every now and again spectacular views to the water and Romania's equally lofty hills. You need to be on foot to appreciate the region fully. Golubac town takes its name from an amazing ruined castle, now partly submerged, that once controlled the upstream end of the Iron Gate gorge. It rises in tiers of picturesque towers on a steep slope direct from the river. No one knows who built it. But it was a Hungarian stronghold in 1337. The Turks captured it soon after the battle of Kosovo (1389), and made it one of their most important frontier fortresses.

About 30 miles from Golubac you come to **Lepenski Vir**, where 21 years of excavations, concluded before most of the site was flooded, unearthed an amazing series of 8 successive prehistoric settlements spanning the 3500 years from 8000 to 4500 BC. They occupied a horseshoe-shaped cwm in the cliffs, and their inhabitants' skills and social organisation proved them far more advanced culturally than most people imagined possible. One thing that archaeologists found striking was that they produced both figures and abstract patterns in their carvings.

Most of the Lepenski Vir finds are now in the Belgrade National Museum. But some are preserved in a museum on the site.

Eight mile so so bring you to **Donji Milanovac** village. It has recently become a popular centre for walking and wildlife enthusiasts. The whole mountainside area above the Danube from Golubac to Kladovo (described below) has recently been made into the Djerdap National Park. Its scenery's stupendous. Its wildlife includes deer of various sorts, wild boar, and wild cat, and even wolf and European bear. Bird raptors include golden eagle, the massive eagle owl, and peregrine. There's also a set of vast limestone caverns near Majdanpek, some 12 miles away across the 2700-foot-high Liškovac hills.

An International Canoeing Regatta is held on the Danube in this area every year.

About 18 miles downstream you reach the **"Kazan"**, the Cauldron that was the gorge's narrowest and most dangerous point. Just where the gorge begins to widen a little there's an inscribed tablet set in virgin rock by the Emperor Trajan in AD 103. It records his rebuilding of a road beside the river, as part of his preparations for the invasion of Dacia (modern Romania), and is always known (in Latin) as **"Tabula Traiana"**. Before the water level rose it was given a higher position. You reach it by a footpath.

Another 15 miles brings you to the massive Yugoslav–Romanian dam that acts also as one of the vast Danube's new crossing-points. The hills have disappeared now, and you're on pretty flat ground again. Cheerful little **Kladovo** town, with a hotel and good restaurants, lies 5–6 miles beyond the dam. Two miles beyond Kladovo you can still see remains of the huge bridge that Trajan's engineers constructed across the river in AD 105.

One of the most exciting excursions possible from Belgrade in summer is a hydrofoil trip down the Danube to Kladovo. Seeing all this from the Danube leaves you feeling dazed.

South of Belgrade

Ten miles south of Belgrade, in the delightful rolling hills and woodlands of the Šumadija region, you come to **Avala** on the old road to Kragujevac. It's bypassed now by Yugoslavia's M1 motorway to Greece. Mount Avala's crowned by the country's WWI memorial to its Unknown Soldier. It's a large mausoleum incorporating vast figures of women in traditional costume from various regions.

Topola, 40 miles further on, marks another national shrine – the home of the insurgent leader the Turks nicknamed Karadjordje (Black George). A large, five-domed church was built in white marble to commemorate him by his grandson, King Petar I of Yugoslavia. Its crypt walls are completely covered with frescos that are copies of many of the Serbian monastery churches' finest paintings.

25 more miles bring you to **Kragujevac**. Today it's the centre of Yugoslavia's rapidly expanding car industry. But its old centre's still lovely and peaceful and closed to powered vehicles. To Yugoslavs however the name recalls mainly the horrifying murder of 7000 of the town's inhabitants, including whole classes of high school pupils and their teachers, on 21 October 1941. They were lined up and machine-gunned by German occupying troops. There's a very moving monument and museum recalling their deaths in the town's Šumarice park.

The high school building is carefully preserved and extremely attractive. Most people also enjoy Kragujevac's very well organised open-air museum and its traditional local houses and craftwork.

The first of the Morava monasteries

East of Kragujevac, on the further side of the M1 motorway and the Great Morava river whose valley it follows, you come to the first of Serbia's great southern monasteries, **Manasija**. Your first sight of it could hardly be more impressive. If there wasn't a church dome standing clear in the middle you'd think it was a castle – which of course it also is.

It's a magnificent piece of work. Its frescos, in particular, are an unusual fusion of Byzantine and Western art. Unfortunately, it was active for barely 20 years before being captured by the Turks. For 400 more years it was constantly fought over and increasingly damaged before being lovingly restored 170 years ago, when Serbia was beginning to be free.

Ravanica monastery, tucked away in another little valley about 15 miles south of Manasija, was built 30 years earlier and completed by Prince Lazar just before his death at the disastrous 1389 Kosovo Polje battle. It too was burned and demolished by the Turks. But the monks fled to the Fruška Gora (see above) with their most precious relics, and founded another Ravanica there. When Austria and Turkey signed the Požarevac Treaty in 1718 which gave this region to Serbia the monks returned and lovingly rebuilt their monastery. Its church is regarded as one of the country's most beautiful. It's built in exceptionally graceful hewn stone and brick.

Gamzigrad

Still further eastward, close now to the Bulgarian border, we come to **Gamzigrad**, on the road to Zaječar and Bulgaria's important Danube port of Vidin. It's the second of Serbia's outstanding Roman sites – a vast fortress even bigger, more magnificent, and even more strongly fortified than Diocletian's great palace at Split (see Chapter 7). It was built by another Emperor, Diocletian's son-in-law, Galerius, for his mother. The attacks of Huns, Goths, Gepids, Avars, and Slavs led to its abandonment some 200 years later. But the foundations, some of the walls, and some staggeringly lovely mosaic floors are still there for everyone to see. The copper mines at Bor, Europe's richest, aren't far off.

Chapter Thirteen

Southern Serbia and Kosovo

In Serbia's southern half the terrain changes. Rolling hills give way to vast mountain massifs like the Proketlje, Zlatibor, Kopaonik, Tara, and Jastrebac massifs. They rise to 9000 feet. There are broad valleys between some of them. Roads (and sometimes railways too) naturally follow them. But to this day there's no easy route out of Serbia between Belgrade and Bosnia-Herzegovina's capital, Sarajevo, less than 200 miles away, except by air.

As a result southern Serbia was a bit less disturbed by the coming and going of migrant tribes and hostile invaders. The remoter side valleys made good hideaways for religious communities looking for peace and quiet. Celts, Romans, Byzantines, Avars, Slavs, and Turks invaded and settled in key points at different times, and Goths and Huns swept through the region. But from medieval days on the monasteries, at least, managed mostly to survive.

Like the northern Vojvodina, the territory of Kosovo, in Serbia's southwest, enjoys self-government. Like the Vojvodina, too, it's ethnically mixed. Official business is conducted in Albanian (the majority language), Serbian, and sometimes Turkish. Unlike the Vojvodina, the region's very mountainous. Yugoslav's highest mountain separates Kosovo and Albania, and its highest mountain pass, the Čakor, over 6000 feet high,

links Kosovo and Montenegro. And unlike the Vojvodina, Kosovo has seen centuries of still-continuing quarrels between its Serb and Albanian populations. But it's an amazingly beautiful corner of the world.

The road to Niš

On the modern M1 motorway Niš is barely three hours from Belgrade. It's worth bearing in mind that it's the second postwar road the Yugoslavs have had to build on this vital route connecting Central Europe with Greece, Bulgaria, Istanbul, and points east. The first, built wholly by hand, soon proved too narrow.

Niš gets its name from the Celtic settlement the Romans called Naissus. It's now Serbia's second city, not a very attractive spot. It lies on flat land with hills all round. Most of what you see today's very modern. But Niš fortress in the town's centre is a Turkish stronghold built on Roman foundations with Roman tombstones, sculpture, columns, and stones. At Medijana, about 3 miles from the town centre, you can see the remains of another magnificent Roman imperial palace. A lot of the objects found there are now in Niš's excellent museum, one of the country's most exciting.

Another museum's a former WWII concentration camp. After a mass escape of about 100 prisoners in 1942

103

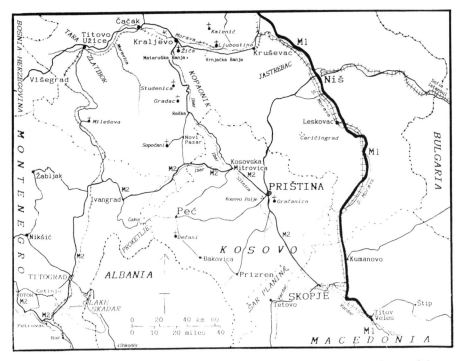

the guards shot 850 of their fellow-captives. And if you want more evidence of human bestiality you can go to the Turkish Čele-kula (Tower of Skulls) in the Military Hospital grounds, a little closer to the town centre than the Roman palace. The heads of 952 Serbs killed in battle were cemented into its walls in 1809 as a warning to other would-be rebels. If you find the Yugoslavs a bit obsessive about the country never being free till 1945 things like this may help to explain why.

The River Nišava's Sičevo gorge near **Niška Banja** (Niš Spa), 6 miles east of Niš, is decidedly colourful. South of the town – you have to travel the 27 miles down the motorway to Leskovac and another 17 WSW on side roads – you can visit the remains of the spectacular Byzantine city of **Caričin Grad**. It was built by the Emperor Justinian in AD 533 to be the capital of

Illyricum Province. But Slav and Avar invaders destroyed it within a century.

North of Niš an important branch road off the M1 motorway turns up the Western Morava (Žapadna Morava) valley. It passes the towns of **Kruševac**, **Kraljevo**, **Čačak**, and **Titovo Užice** before crossing the mountains to Višegrad in Bosnia-Herzegovina (Chapter 16). Little known to foreigners, this part of central Serbia offers some magnificent scenery.

Fascinating spas, such as **Vrnjačka Banja** and **Mataruška Banja**, lie south of the road between Kruševac and Kraljevo. Further south from Kraljevo, on the border between Serbia proper and Kosovo, the **Kopaonik** mountain range rising to almost 7000 feet and rich in forests and spas shelters an increasingly popular winter-and-summer resort at Suvo Ridište. **Mount Maljen**, some 35

104

miles northwest of Čačak, is famous for its fields of wild narcissus and the light entertainment White Narcissus Festival held in May. The **Zvijezda National Park** 10 miles west of Titovo Užice contains rich forests, rare flora, part of the River Drina's canyon (Chapter 16), and wildlife that includes bears. South of Titovo Užice, on **Mount Zlatibor** 3000-foot high plateau, Partizanske Vode is the centre of a mountain resort which can boast 2000 hours of sun a year, as well as lovely, gentle scenery.

The monasteries

The medieval monasteries in side valleys off the Western Morava and Ibar main valleys are the chief glory of southern Serbia. If you're lucky you may still find one or two coach tours operating to them. If not, your only hope is to hire a car for a week or two and buy a good map. If you've any feeling for art, and if you enjoy good scenery you'll not regret it.

The richness of Byzantine and early Serbian art and architecture is still hardly known to Westerners. Its traditions seems strange. Its treasures – buildings, paintings, embroideries, jewellery, carvings, and illuminated books – are waiting to be discovered.

Žiča monastery, near the town of Kraljevo at the junction of the Rivers Ibar and Western Morava, is one of the more accessible. It's also considered one of Yugoslavia's most important historical buildings.

The monastery was founded soon after 1200, and in 1219 became the first seat of the newly independent Serbian Orthodox Church. It has been destroyed and carefully restored several times. Its last restoration was completed in 1976, after WWII damage. But most of the monastery

complex, including its walls, still keeps its original form. Its original royal charter, inscribed in fresco, is still in place over the church door. Its frescos were painted in the 13th and 14th centuries. The later ones are particularly fine.

Nuns occupy Žiča now. On Sundays you'll be welcome at the morning liturgy, which starts at about 9 am and lasts up to two hours. You'll find the little church's rich iconostasis, the icons and oil lamps, the incense and bells, and the priest's, deacon's and nuns' plainchant strangely moving. Orthodox churches don't have seats. If you want to walk round, or go away before the service ends, or come in late, no one will be offended.

Ljubostinja, two miles north of the Kraljevo–Kruševac road from the village of Trstenik, was built by Princess Milica after her husband, Prince Lazar, had been killed at Kosovo Polje (below) in 1389. Its church, built in carved stone, is particularly attractive. Some of its wall-paintings are outstanding.

Kalenić, 20 miles north, tucked away in the hills and reached by poor roads, is also renowned for its beautiful architecture and fine 15th-century murals. You'll find UNESCO-listed **Studenica** in a side valley some 7 miles west of a little town called Ušće, 32 miles up the Ibar from Kraljevo. It dates from 1197 and once included 13 churches. The frescos, again, are important examples of 13th-century Serbian art. **Gradac** lies in another side valley, some 10 miles south of Studenica.

The little town of Ras, now destroyed, gave its name to the "Raška" architectural style used by all these Ibar valley religious houses. A 13-mile drive from modern **Raška** town brings you to **Novi Pazar**, whose name means Newmarket. A Turkish fort stands in the middle of the town, close to a typical Turkish 18th-century caravanserai, not far from the elegant Altun-Alem 15th-century mosque, with its soaring minaret. The Ibar, incidentally, provides good fishing and canoeing.

About three miles north of Novi Pazar you'll see at the roadside the tiny, simple church of St Peter and St Paul, built 1000 years ago, and linked to major events at the founding of Serbia's medieval Kingdom. It's Yugoslavia's oldest still-functioning Orthodox church.

Novi Pazar also provides your base for visits to **Sopoćani** monastery, 10 miles southwest. It was founded by King Uroš I in 1265–75, when Serbia's trade was prosperous and widespread, as a mausoleum for his mother. She was a granddaughter of the Venetian doge, Giovanni Dandolo. Less than half the original 13th-century frescos have survived continuous burnings and pillage – after a complete restoration in 1928 the church was actually used as stables by German troops during WWII. Nevertheless, they and the church's architecture have been judged so outstanding that it features on UNESCO's heritage list.

Lovely **Mileševa** lies hidden in mountains over 60 miles west of Novi Pazar. It's best reached from the Titovo Užice–Titograd road. St Sava, Serbia's first patriarch, is buried here.

These are by no means all of Serbia's medieval monasteries. They're just some of the more important. You'll find lots more scattered throughout the mountains. The spectacular **Ovčar-Kablar** gorge (Ovčarska-Kablarska klisura) west of Titovo

Užice alone contains 8 on both banks of the Western Morava.

Kosovo

Kosovo's a strange and exotic self-governing region southwest of Niš. It's shut in by high mountains, and reached by only four major roads. Its sole major towns are its capital, Priština, and Prizren, Peć, and Titova Mitrovica. Its area's a fifth of Serbia proper's (without the Vojvodina and Kosovo). Yet its population's nearly a third as large. In many parts its scenery's exceptionally lovely. But it's Yugoslavia's poorest and most unhappy region.

Albanians lived here long before strict national frontiers existed. After the Turkish invasion most were converted to Islam, as Albania had been. The Serbs weren't. In fact, the Serbian Orthodox Church's headquarters, the Patriarchate, was moved to Peć in Kosovo in 1346, 43 years before the battle of Kosovo Polje, and remained there till 1766. Lots of ordinary Serbs however became refugees in northern Serbia. When the Turks were forced to abandon Serbia in 1878 Serbs began returning. To them Kosovo was "home". But Albanians who'd been there all along thought them intruders.

The quarrel still goes on, exacerbated by virulent propaganda from Albanian radio just over the border and expatriates in Europe. Its real basis, one can't help thinking, is poverty. Kosovo is Yugoslavia's poorest region. No matter how much money from Yugoslav and international funds pours into Kosovo its living standards never improve compared with the rest of Yugoslavia. And the Muslim population goes on increasing faster than the rest of the region's (Albanian families average over 6 children, compared with up to 2½ elsewhere in Yugoslavia). The economic parallels with Ulster seem clear – especially when you know the poverty of Belfast's Shankhill and Falls areas.

The Kosovo plain around Priština and the "Church Land" (Metohija) near Peć are Kosovo's main flat areas. The Province's official title used to be Kosovo i Metojia (Kosovo and the Church Land), abbreviated Kosmet. It's called Kosovo today.

Major roads from Niš and Kraljevo (with a branch from Titova Mitrovica leading to Titograd in Montenegro) take you to **Priština**, Kosovo's capital. At first glance Priština seems an almost wholly modern city. It isn't. It has 13 mosques (two of them well over 500 years old and beautifully built), two sets of baths dating from Turkish times, a Turkish clocktower, a considerable number of old houses, some going back 500 years, and several Orthodox churches. Its Kosovo Museum contains a superb collection of local prehistoric, Greek, and Roman statuary, jewellery from all periods, and a fine Turkish collection.

About 3 miles west of Priština you come to the scene of the 1389 battle of **Kosovo Polje**, with the Monument to the Heroes of Kosovo, built in 1953, and the Gazi Mestan tomb, containing two unnamed Turks, buried there after the battle. Both commanders were also killed. Murat's buried in an elegant tomb out on the road to Titova Mitrovica. Prince Lazar lies in Ravanica monastery (Chapter 12).

Gračanica, 5 miles south of Priština, strikes many as the loveliest of all Serbia's monasteries. There's an exact copy of it in Belgrade, known as St Mark's (Sveti Marko).

Of Kosovo's other towns, **Prizren**, 47 miles southwest of Priština and reached by surfaced side roads, is still very Turkish in appearance. It was once one of the Balkans' largest towns, still famous for its gold and silver work. **Titova Mitrovica** today is largely industrial, with the nearby Trepca mines containing Europe's richest lead and zinc deposits.

Magnificently-sited **Peć** mixes Turkish and Christian remains. In the town you can see the Bajrakli and other mosques. Turkish public baths, several Turkish notables' homes, an old mill, and several Albanian tower houses, built for protection like those of Scotland and elsewhere.

Just west of the town, almost at the beginning of the White Drim's (Beli Drim's) spectacular **Rugovo gorge** flanked by thickly wooded Proketlje's mountain slopes leading to the 6000-foot Čakor pass into Montenegro, you come to one of the loveliest of all Yugoslavia's collections of Orthodox churches – the many-domed **Peć Patriarchate** (Pećka Patriarhija), as it's always called. The oldest church, dedicated to the Holy Apostles, contains striking frescos in an ascetic, monastic style, unlike the humanism of Sopoćani and other monasteries. Three later churches were built onto it. The Patriarchate's Treasury contains fine icons and plate. But the place's real delight is its fantastic position below the towering forested mountains.

Dečani monastery (Visoki Dečani), 10 miles south of Peć on the road to Prizren (above), clings to the lower slopes of Mount Djeravica, Yugoslavia's highest peak, part of the vast **Proketlje** range. Its unusually large church contains frescoes representing over 10,000 figures. The region's famous also for its chestnut forests and the Dečanska Bistrica's gorge. Local wildlife includes bear, wild boar, and lynx.

Chapter Fourteen

Macedonia

Your main memories of a summer stay in Macedonia will be of heat, greenery, and red roofs. It's the most southerly of Yugoslavia's Republics. Its neighbours are Serbia, Kosovo, Greece, Albania, and Bulgaria. If you go in winter, however, your impressions will be very different. Macedonia's a land of mountains. No less than 34 peaks top 6500 feet, and the highest reaches almost 9000. There are only three small areas of flat land. Of its three lovely large mountain lakes, Macedonia shares Dojran in the east with Greece, Prespa with Greece and Albania, and Ohrid with Albania.

You'll notice that many older houses are built in a distinctive style. The Macedonians are a separate nation, with a language and culture of their own. Under Alexander the Great (died 323 BC) their rule extended as far as India. Today, they're divided between Yugoslavia, Bulgaria, and Turkey. In addition to the usual history of invasion by Greeks, Romans, Byzantines, Goths, Avars, Slavs, Turks, Italians, Germans, Bulgarians, and many others, Yugoslav Macedonia still has occasional claims made on its territory by modern Bulgaria. No one seems to take them too seriously. It's a pleasant, contented land, even though there are people still alive there who remember not only all the bitter fighting of 1941–45 and the civil wars that accompanied it but also of the Balkan War of 1912 that precipitated the Turks' final withdrawal after more than 5 centuries of occupation.

Skopje

Macedonia's fine capital, **Skopje** (also spelled Skoplje), has been an important settlement on Central Europe's connecting route to the Aegean for 6000 years. The hilltop fort dominating town and Vardar valley, which road and railway still have to follow, was probably built in the 6th–7th centuries by Byzantine forces trying to hold off invading Pechenegs, Polovtzians, Normans, Bulgars, and Slavs. It was given up by the military and made into a public park only after the last war's end.

Apart from its mountain-ringed riverside position, Skopje's main attraction is its wonderful array of ancient Turkish buildings. Many are still in everyday use. The bazaar (Turkish market), for instance, contains over 1000 small shops in traditional Turkish style – though there were over twice that number 400 years ago. Three old caravanserais (merchants' inns) can still be seen in the bazaar. You can visit Mustapha Pasha's beautiful mosque, built in 1492, and several other mosques in the town, and cross the wide river (on foot only) by a stone bridge even older than Mustapha Pasha's mosque. Fine public baths and tombs have also survived from Turkish times, despite an Austrian general's partly successful attempt to burn the town down in 1689 and the devastation caused by the 1963 earthquake.

Many new buildings, such as Skopje's National Theatre, match the beauty of the old. The Museums of Macedonia (Archaeological, Ethnological, and Historical) contain magnificent and highly important collections. They were formed from the National Museum founded in 1945. At the tiny Sveti Spas (Holy Saviour) church in the town you can see some staggering 19th-century woodcarving.

Just outside Skopje, **Nerezi** monastery's little church, dedicated to St Panteleimon, contains outstanding 12th-century frescos. It's located on Mount Vodno, high above the town. An evening drink in Vodno, on a terrace looking north across the town to the mountains beyond while the red sun's setting and the lights are coming on, is an experience you'll not easily forget.

Other important monasteries near Skopje include **Matka** (6 miles west), **St Nikita** (9 miles north), and **Markov** (11 miles south). They're all tucked away in the hills and the journeys to them are part of their attraction.

Some other towns

Kumanovo, just off the M1 motorway 20 miles north of Skopje, is one of Macedonia's many ancient towns. It's mostly famous however as the jumping-off point for trips to the **Staro Nagoričine** monastery to its northeast. It has magnificent 14th century frescos.

30 miles southeast of Skopje you come to **Titov Veles**. It's a colourfully jumbled little town that has recently become an industrial centre. Excavations begun in 1924 are still going on at **Stobi**, 11 miles further down the Vardar valley. This is a very ancient city, known to have existed in 197 BC but not mentioned at all after AD 1014. Vast city walls, a Roman amphitheatre, mosaic floors, frescos, and innumerable other items have been unearthed so far.

South of Titov Veles the Vardar flows through the spectacular **Demir Kaplja** gorge, one of 4 on its relatively short course.

A right turn from Stobi takes you to to **Prilep** (35 miles), on the edge of the relatively large Pelagonian plain. If you're really exploring Macedonia, take the narrow surfaced road west to **Kruševo**. Here you'll see fine examples of traditional Macedonian houses, built largely in wood, with woodcarvings and overhanging upper storeys. If you follow the road south from Kruševo you come to a fine new road and can turn right for almost wholly modern **Kičevo,** 42 miles from Kruševo, and for **Tetovo**, a similar distance from Kičevo. Tetovo looks pretty modern today. But it contains another fine mixture of Turkish buildings and ancient Orthodox churches.

On the first part of this road you've the vast **Mavrovo** mountain massif and Mavrovo National Park and lake (see below) on your left. If you turn sharp left for Mavrovi Hanovi (Mavrovo Inns) 5 miles before you reach Gostivar you can follow a surfaced road to the little village of **Galičnik,** over 4000 feet up in the hills.

Galičnik folk were famous for their painting and woodcarving. But they had almost all left the village in 1971. After 1975 however people started

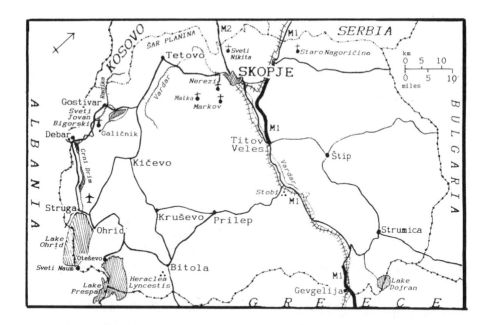

determinedly returning. They renovated their traditional hillside homes, and turned the village into a mountain resort. Galičnik had always been famous for the colourfulness of its wedding traditions and costumes. Now they put them on in all their glory for visitors every August.

30 miles beyond Prilep on the road from Stobi you reach **Bitola**, at the Pelagonian plain's southern end. Under the Turks Bitola's tobacco trade made it well known to merchants in London, Paris, Vienna, and Leipzig. Foreign countries maintained consulates there. Many old buildings have survived.

Just southwest of Bitola, too, you'll find the magnificent remains of **Heraclea Lyncestis**, believed to have been founded by Philip II of Macedon, Alexander the Great's father. Staggeringly beautiful Roman mosaic floors, parts of the city's fortifications,

and remains of many buildings are still there. The highly important model of Phidias' Athena Promachos which you can see in Belgrade's National Museum (Chapter 12) was found here.

Ohrid and its lake

If you turn west at Bitola, a typical and very lovely mountain road takes you past the Pelister and Galičica National Parks (see below). A side road also takes you to **Lake Prespa**, nearly 3000 feet above sea level. It has 8500-foot Pelister on one side and 6000-foot Galičica on the other. Part belongs to Albania, and part to Greece. The western shore has some fine sandy beaches. Summer resorts are being developed at **Oteševo** and elsewhere, close to the Albanian border. The lake provides excellent fishing. Its water drains westward into Lake Ohrid by underground channels.

After 45 miles you reach **Ohrid** town,

110

one of 4 Yugoslav towns declared by UNESCO to be of world heritage importance. Its old centre, set out in a natural amphitheatre, slopes down to the lake, over 2000 feet above the sea. It consists largely of fine Macedonian houses. Two of the most impressive have been made into a museum. There are three mosques in the town, one with a former dervish monastery beside it. The well-preserved vast fort immediately above the town – you can explore it if you've the energy to climb the hill – is known to have withstood Goth attacks in AD 497.

But it's Ohrid's churches and religious remains that make it of world importance. After Saints Cyril and Methodius had converted many Slavs to Christianity in the 9th century, Saint Clement and Saint Naum continued the work from Ohrid. The town became a sort of Slav religious university. Many staggeringly beautiful churches were built in and near it.

One of the oldest is St Sophia (Sveta Sofija), close to the lake. It was built around 1050. Its frescos date from the 11th, 12th, and 14th centuries. The loveliest church, most people agree, is St Clement's (Sveti Kliment). It was originally dedicated to St Mary Peribleptos (the Glorious Virgin Mary). It came to be known as St Clement's when the saint's remains were transferred here from an older church, now in ruins, that he himself had rebuilt. St Clement's frescos are masterpieces. They're the work of three painters well known in their day, whose work has survived elsewhere. The church boasts also one of the world's best collections of icons.

You'll find the region's two most picturesque churches outside the town. Both are tiny. One's Sveti Jovan Kaneo (St John of Kaneo), perched on a craggy cliff above the lake-fishing village of Kaneo. It was built in the 13th century. The other's at Lake Ohrid's further end, right on the Albanian border. You reach it by boat or by road. It was built in the 9th century, and is dedicated to St Naum. Its carved bronze sanctuary doors are magnificent. You can visit a dozen or more churches, none less than 500 years old in or near Ohrid.

The town also possesses modern resort hotels 3–5 miles from the town on the lake's shores. Both have shingly beaches backed by trees and bus services into the town. Tennis is available at the Hotel Metropol. UK packages fly you to Ohrid's own airport with a change of planes at Ljubljana.

Struga, close to Ohrid's airport, is another pleasant lakeside town, about 8 miles west of Ohrid. The Crni Drim river (Black Drim) drains northward out of Lake Ohrid to flow through Albania into the Adriatic. Struga lies at the southern end of the road running close to the Albanian frontier that we took on our way to Galičnik. The road goes through **Debar**, another of Macedonia's ancient settlements. It also passes the well-preserved monastery of **Sveti Jovan Bigorski** (St John Bigorski), perched on a steep slope in the Radika gorge below the Jablanica mountain ridge whose summits mark the modern frontier with Albania.

National Parks, wildlife, and the open air

We've already mentioned Macedonia's three National Parks – Mavrovo, Pelister, and Galičica. **Mavrovo** is Yugoslavia's largest National Park. Apart from its large artificial lake and the Radika gorge, Mavrovo's covered with beech, fir, and spruce forest. There's plenty of trout in its rivers. Bear, chamois, lynx, deer, and fox can be shot (or just watched) in its forests. A cable car operates from Mavrovo village to the Mount Bistra ski slopes in winter.

Pelister stretches from Lake Prespa to the Pelagonia plain. Its wildlife includes bear, wild boar, chamois, and partridge, as well as a rare type of black pine. You can enjoy cross-country skiing on its gentle slopes in winter.

Galičica, between Lake Prespa and Lake Ohrid, is famous for its tree and plant species – 230 in all. There are broad mountain meadows and pastures on its heights. Its fauna includes lynx, wolf, and eagle.

You can also ski at **Popova Šapka**, reached by cable car from Tetovo. It's part of the vast Šar Planina massif that separates Macedonia from Kosovo.

On **Lake Dojran**, some 20 miles from the Greek frontier crossing at Gevgelija, cormorants are still used to help catch the lake's extremely plentiful fish. Surrounding woodlands include figs, almond, sesame, elm, oak, ash, beech, and maple. They're inhabited by wild boar, jackal, and other creatures.

Chapter Fifteen

Inland Montenegro

Montenegro's the smallest of Yugoslavia's Republics. It occupies a twentieth of the country's area and holds little more than a fortieth of its population. If you look at the map you'll see why. It's nearly all mountain. The scenery's stupendous. Even arriving by air at Titograd airport in what's virtually Montenegro's only flat area gives you magnificent views – providing it's done in daylight.

We've already had a quick glance at most of the Republic's inland regions when dealing with excursions from its coast resorts (see Chapter 9). But some of this needs filling out – particularly since it's now possible to buy packages that take you direct to Cetinje, Montenegro's former capital (Chapter 9), and Žabljak, your touring base for the superb Durmitor National Park.

Titograd and its origins

Although **Titograd** looks a pretty well totally modern town historical documents make it clear that there was a Roman settlement called Alata (or Halata) exactly where Titograd now stands, and that by the 12th century it was known as Podgorica. Given that it's located in the middle of what's almost Montenegro's only flat land it's hardly surprising that other major settlements have also been discovered close to the city.

These include a pre-Roman Illyrian settlement fortified with the huge "Cyclopean" squared-off stone blocks which it seems could never have been moved without ropes and all sorts of equipment that simply didn't exist when the walls were put up. Just north of Titograd a large Roman town called Doclea has been unearthed. It seems to have been destroyed by invaders in 602. But it gave its name, in the form Duklija, to an early version of what eventually became the Kingdom of Montenegro. Fine glass from Doclea and a lot of other fascinating prehistoric and early items can be seen in Titograd Town Museum's archaeological section.

Canyons and National Parks

If you drive around in Kosovo, Macedonia, and Montenegro you begin to feel that an awful lot of Yugoslavia consists of mountain gorges with roads at the bottom of them. The canyon that the short **River Morača** flows through on its way to Titograd and Lake Skadar (see Chapter 9), and from there through Albania to the sea, certainly isn't one you'll easily forget. Its near-vertical sides average just on 2000 feet. At one point the river flows at the foot of an enormous bare rocky cliff. The Belgrade–Bar railway runs through the gorge.

The **Tara** near its source flows in the opposite direction in a roughly parallel valley. About 60 miles from Titograd it

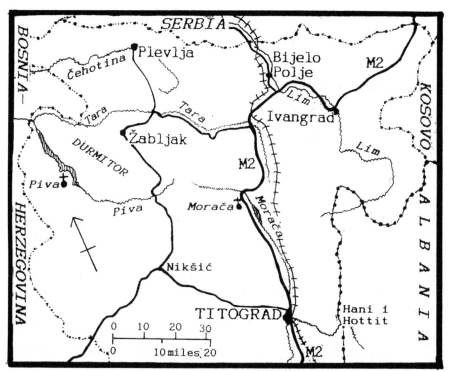

has the **Biogradsko National Park** on its right bank. One of the park's main attractions is glacial Lake Biogradsko, surrounded by the dense forests that cover 85% of its 10,000 acres. Their altitude varies from 3000 to 7000 feet. The park contains a huge variety of fully protected plants. Your best jumping-off point for exploring the area is Kolašin, about 10 miles away.

East of the huge Durmitor mountain mass the Tara's confined in another spectacular canyon whose height's even greater than the Morača gorge's. It's second, in fact, only to Colorado's Grand Canyon. The river provides good fishing and excellent canoeing. You have to drive through its canyon on your way to **Žabljak**, your centre for exploring the breathtaking **Durmitor National Park**. Whereas Biogradsko has been organised as a European-style conservation area,

where nature's simply left undisturbed, the Durmitor park's run American-style (to quote the Yugoslavs), with good accommodation and all sorts of recreational possibilities.

It's an amazing region. 15 of its peaks rise over 6500 feet. It's bounded to the west by yet another amazing canyon, made by the **River Piva**, which is now a long, peaceful lake, thanks to an enormous hydro-electric dam. Durmitor has 20 glacial and karst lakes at heights between 4000 and 6500 feet. And the whole's set against a wonderful pine forest background. All sorts of fish and game are abundant. Hunting (at a price) and fishing are permitted. Motorable tracks go to all main points and the entire region's intersected by well-marked, well-maintained footpaths. Three ski-lifts give it the beginnings of a worthwhile ski resort. Hotels, chalets, and campsites are

114

strategically placed. Your base, little Žabljak town, stands nearly 5000 feet above the sea – Yugoslavia's highest settlement. You reach it by a modern asphalted road.

Yet another colourful canyon has been cut by the **River Lim** on its way to join the Drina (Chapter 16) from its source above Lake Plav in the Proketlje range (Chapter 13). It's popular with anglers and kayak enthusiasts, and there are good sandy beaches in the gorge.

Towns and monasteries

Perhaps we should mention two more outstanding monasteries. **Morača,** near Kolašin, built in 1252 in a magnificent part of the Morača canyon near the Svetigora waterfall, and **Piva**, near the River Piva's source. Piva had to be moved lock, stock, and barrel (including 10,000 square feet of frescos) to a higher position when the river was dammed, turning another fine gorge into a long lake. You can see more notable frescos in Morača monastery's

church. Piva's rich store of early books and gold and silver plate includes a recently-discovered psalter produced before 1500 – only a few years after printing was invented – by the Crnojević printing press in Cetinje (Chapter 9).

Though we've not yet mentioned them, towns other than Titograd and Cetinje do exist in inland Montenegro. You reach **Plevlja**, near where the borders of Montenegro, Serbia, and Bosnia-Herzegovina meet, by a very scenic mountain side road. The town can boast an impressive mosque and a delightful small monastery, both from the 16th century. **Bijelo Polje**, on the main M2's inland section that also forms part of the route from Belgrade to Titograd, has another wonderful mountain setting. **Nikšić**, 37 miles northwest of Titograd, is Montenegro's most densely-populated commune. The town's mostly modern. But you can climb up to the picturesque ruins of an ancient hilltop castle above it. You'll find the view over the flat River Zeta valley, surrounded by mountains worth the effort.

Chapter Sixteen

Bosnia-Herzegovina

Bosnia-Herzegovina's one of Yugoslavia's largest Republics, almost equal in size to Serbia without the Vojvodina and Kosovo, or to Croatia. But its territory consists almost wholly of mountains. Every now and again a "polje" appears – a fertile hollow in the hills with a town in its middle or at its edge. The rivers flow mostly in gorges or steep valleys that are often magnificently forested. Two or three miles of beeches in their glorious autumn colours can be pretty overpowering. Imagine, if you can, the impact of the 150-mile drive from Bosnia-Herzegovina's capital, Sarajevo, to Dubrovnik by the inland road (via Tjentište and Gacko) with a full array of fall colours draped down miles of steep mountainsides for a good two-thirds of the distance.

Before we go further we'd better get the Republic's name clear. Yugoslavs call it Bosna i Hercegovina (Bosnia and Herzegovina), and abbreviate it BiH. We abbreviate it Bosnia-Herzegovina to make it clear we're dealing with a single area, not two – Croatia and Bosnia and Herzegovina sounds like three regions. And we use the German-Austrian spelling Herzegovina because we're more accustomed to pronouncing z as ts (normal in German) than to having c sounded that way (normal in Yugoslav languages). Bosnia takes its name from the River Bosna, which flows through it. Hercegovina means

"County" (herceg in the Yugoslav languages = count: the German equivalent is Herzog).

The Republic's early history's similar to most of Yugoslavia's. When the invading Slavs began to group themelves into settled kingdoms Bosnia was linked first with Serbia, and then with Duklja, based in what's now Montenegro (Chapter 15). Then it came under the sway of the Hungarian-Croat monarchs, who established it as a "county" (herceg's an originally Hungarian word).

Turks occupied it from 1463 to 1878. A lot of the local population were converted to Islam, and over a million of their descendants still are Muslims. When the Turks were forced to abandon most of their European possessions the Congress of Berlin decided that Bosnia-Herzegovina should be Austrian. The Bosnians resisted. Annexation wasn't really complete till 1908. Six years later the murder in Sarajevo of the Austrian Crown Prince by a young Bosnian patriot sparked Austria's attack on Serbia, accused of helping the Bosnians. WWI was the result.

As if this background of foreign occupation and violence weren't enough, Bosnia-Herzegovina's mountain fastnesses were the scene of some of WWII's most violent fighting and its most hideous atrocities. In a single act (one of many) 120 villages were burned as reprisals for help given the Partisans (Chapter 17). It's extraordinary to think of all this happening in a region of such extraordinary beauty.

Mostar

In Chapter 7 we mentioned excursions from the coast to Mostar. But we didn't describe the town or the road you reach it by.

Beyond Počitelj, the picturesque little former Turkish frontier post (Chapter 7), road and railway follow the peaceful River Neretva, flowing through a mainly rich and fertile hilly countryside. At Buna village, about 15 miles from Pičitelj, it's worth making a few miles détour to **Blagaj na Buni** (Blagaj-on-Buna).

Like the Ombla near Dubrovnik (Chapter 8) and the waterfalls beside the Gulf of Kotor (Chapter 9), the River Buna pours straight out of the base of an enormous bare rocky cliff. On top of the cliff you can see the ruins of a citadel fortress that was actually the region's capital for many centuries, and was abandoned by the Turks only in 1835. The village at the foot of the cliff is still almost purely Turkish. It includes three mosques, some finely decorated private houses, several ancient watermills, a 16th-century stone bridge, and remains of a "musafirhana", a sort of Muslim spike, where impecunious travellers were given free board and lodging.

Blagaj was also one of Europe's very few places whose native vines weren't wiped out by the 1863 phylloxera epidemic (we had to be restocked from America). The Žilavka grapes that survived in Blagaj produce a wonderful, fruity, rather heavy white wine. Unfortunately, what's widely sold as Žilavka in Yugoslavia doesn't

come from Blagaj. It's just a heavy wine made, one supposes, from Žilavka grapes.

Mostar, 7 miles away, occupies a magnificent position astride the Nerevta, with mountains on either side and in the distance. Its centre is almost purely Turkish, its suburbs European and modern. You see the minarets of several mosques as you approach the town. The much-photographed Old Bridge, however, is the point everyone makes for first. It was built in 1566, in stone, in honour of the Sultan, Suleiman the Magnificent, renowned for his buildings throughout Turkey's empire. With its guardhouses at either end and a great hump in its roadway, it makes as picturesque a photo as anyone could want. The carefully-restored Old Bazaar (Stara čaršija) of tiny Turkish shops leads from the bridge.

You can go into several old mosques and see the interiors of some well-preserved Turkish houses. The Karadjoz Bey mosque and the Biščević house, which projects over the river, are perhaps the most impressive. There's also a tiny Orthodox church, built below ground level, which has a separate gallery for women, divided from the men by a grill in the Turkish manner.

From Počitelj you can also strike westward to Čitluk and the little village of **Medjugorje**. It has attracted a lot of visitors recently because the Virgin Mary is seen regularly by a village girl.

On to Sarajevo

Within a few miles of Mostar, still following the Neretva, you come to yet another of Yugoslavia's magnificent river gorges. When you emerge from it at **Jablanica**, you find the road gets

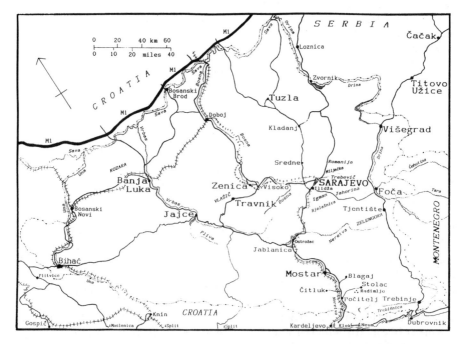

out of the Neretva valley by a tunnel. It's worth stopping half an hour in Jablanica however to see one of Yugoslavia's most unusual modern museums. It commemorates the 1943 Battle of the Wounded, and includes a railway bridge that has obviously been blown up and left lying deep down in the river. When a large Partisan force was surrounded, Tito fooled the Germans by blowing up the bridge which was their only escape route. They left the bridge unguarded. But it was patched overnight. The entire force escaped. So did the wounded.

A second road tunnel takes you to **Ostrožac**, overlooking the huge Jablanica artificial lake. It's designed to supply power to the whole region and water to places as far away as Korčula island (Chapter 9). Restaurants that give you a fine view of the mountain-ringed lake make a good coffee- or lunch-stop.

A little over 40 miles brings you to the turning for **Ilidža**, a remarkably green and fertile spot in the middle of endless mountain heights. However hot the sun Ilidža's always cool. The reason's the cold water surging from innumerable springs. It's an extraordinary flat area, planted with masses of trees and flowering shrubs, and intersected by fast-flowing streams. There are hotels here which save you from the summer heat of nearby Sarajevo. It's a favourite relaxation spot for people from the big city.

Sarajevo

Sarajevo itself occupies a wonderful position at the foot of high mountains athwart the River Miljačka. You get a tremendous view of it from the top of the cablecar that takes you onto Mount Trebević. It's a city of 500,000 inhabitants.

118

In character it's wonderfully mixed. There are mosques galore, a superbly-restored old covered market, the Bruza Bezistan, now filled with boutiques, the old coppersmiths' bazaar (Kazandžiska čaršija), where copperworkers carry on their trade in the traditional way though many shops inevitably cater also for tourists, the main bazaar (baščaršija), a Muslim monastery, and an imaret, a sort of public social service cookhouse.

The Moriča Han (inn), dating from about 1700, has been turned into an extremely good and colourful restaurant. In its heyday it had rooms for 300 guests, storerooms for the merchandise they were carrying, and stabling for their horses. The domed Daira, which once held 9 shops facing an enclosed courtyard, is also now a restaurant. It serves a very special Bosnian stew in attractive large individual earthenware pots that's indistinguishable from Lancashire hotpot. Most dishes are rather more exotic.

Several mosques are still in use, and many Muslim families occupy traditional Turkish-style houses scattered mainly over steep hillsides above the town centre – you see them on the way up to Mount Trebević. But Sarajevo's a long way today from being purely Turkish.

The Austrians left ostentatious traces of their 40-year occupation (1878–1918). The astonishing former Town Hall (now the National Library of Bosnia–Herzegovina) was built in a peculiar Moorish style, overlooking the Neretva. Why Moorish? Presumably anything vaguely eastern was alright for a city considered wholly Oriental in 1878.

Downstream from the former Town Hall you'll find two cement blocks with footprints marking the spot where the young patriot Gavril Princip stood in 1914 when he shot the Austrian Crown Prince and sparked off the First World War.

In Sarajevo you can also see both Turkish and Jewish burial grounds, a Jewish synagogue that now contains the Republic's Hebrew Museum, and an Orthodox church of unknown date. Remains of the fortified storehouse which Dubrovnik merchants used are still visible. The great Turkish traveller Eveliya Chelebi wrote in 1664: "All kinds of goods from India, Arabia, Persia, Poland, and Czechoslovakia can be bought here very cheaply . . . Dubrovnik and Venice are only two to three days journey from this town . . . goods can be brought here on packhorses from Zadar, Šibenik, and Split. Expensive wool and fine slik materials . . ."

Sarajevo's modern shops and boutiques are still very attractive. Skenderija, the sports centre which hosted the 1984 Winter Olympics' skating, is a tiptop example of modern architecture. An efficient bus and railway station has been built southwest of the town centre. The airport near Ilidža has links to all Yugoslavia's main cities. And on the **Trebević–Jahorina** and **Igman–Bjelašnica** mountains, 5–20 miles from the town, you've a good choice of hotels, custom-built for the 1984 Winter Olympics and for subsequent all-year-round visitors. With swimming pools, dancing, tennis, excellent mountain walking, and regular buses into the town they offer a lot of advantages. Deep down among high mountains, Sarajevo can be exceedingly hot and stuffy in summer.

Jahorina and Bjelašnica rise to over

6000 feet. Jahorina's roughly 10 miles wide and almost 20 long. Pines shroud the slopes up to 5000 feet. There are vast grassy slopes above them. The area has been declared a nature reserve. Bjelašnica's bare and rugged to its south, but covered with pine forests almost to the summit on its north and northwestern sides.

Sarajevo to Dubrovnik

The inland route to Dubrovnik gives you a memorable view of typical Bosnian scenery – and also allows you to see the superb Sutjeska National Park. Your chief problem's locating the turning near Ilidža which takes you to Trnovo and Brod, where you join the main Belgrade–Čačak–Foča–Dubrovnik road. Once safely started you've only road and scenery to cope with.

You're very quickly into a series of deep V-shaped valleys whose slopes are covered largely with beeches that turn fantastic colours in autumn. After 70-odd miles, when you're feeling completely stunned, you find yourself in the little rather Alpine-looking village of **Tjentište** in the **Sutjeska** National Park. Beyond it you see the massive memorial commemorating the Sutjeska battle of 1943. Of 19,700 Partisans, including 4000 wounded, 7356 were killed. The memorial's an amazing, huge abstract work that seems to move and flow as you drive by. Unfortunately, it was constructed in concrete and has for some time been showing signs of wear.

Majestic mountains rise all around, including the vast Zelengora (Green Mountain). Their peaks soar to 7500 feet, and they're covered with dense woodlands that include Europe's largest surviving virgin forest. Several mountain lakes are scattered among

them. There's a hotel close to the memorial and shops in the friendly village. Marked paths guide you through the hills and woods. The walking can be strenuous because of steepness. Partly because of historical associations and partly for wildlife considerations the region has been declared a National Park.

There's more striking mountain scenery on the way to Dubrovnik. The road's anything but flat, and it's unfortunately used by more heavy traffic than it was built for. Sometimes it gets a bit potholed. And there are segments when you can find yourself driving close to steep, long slopes. But it's worth the effort. Or you can catch a bus.

At **Trebinje**, 20 miles before Dubrovnik, you can see a very attractive Turkish bridge over the River Trebišnjica – the one that disappears near Hutovo and reappears at Dubrovnik's Ombla (Chapter 8). There are also several mosques, an old Turkish clocktower, and some typically Turkish town houses – all hidden among the tall buildings of what's now an attractive, thriving modern town. You cross the former Turkish frontier less than 5 miles from Dubrovnik. It's still the unnoticeable dividing line between Bosnia and Croatia.

On this route, if you turn left (northeast) at Brod you can follow the River Drina's winding mountain valley to **Foča, Goražde,** and **Višegrad,** where you leave the Drina and cross into Serbia to follow the Western Morava to Titovo Užice, Čačak, Kraljevo and, if you wish, Belgrade (Chapter 12). Višegrad's the most striking of these towns. It's the setting for Nobel Prizewinner Ivo Andrić's novel "The Bridge Over The River

Drina". The magnificent 11-span Turkish bridge built in 1578 is still there. The Drina's formed by the Tara and Piva shortly after they leave the valleys below Mount Durmitor (Chapter 15). The section between Foča and Goražde, in particular, offers trips on rafts, and much of the river's extremely popular with canoeists.

The roads to Belgrade

Apart from the route through Foča just mentioned, you've a choice of two other very cross-country routes. You can leave by the road that passes through **Romanija**, a mountain resort long popular with Sarajevo folk, and continue through Vlasenica, Zvornik, and Šabac to the Zagreb–Belgrade M1 motorway about 10 miles east of Sremska Mitrovica (Chapter 11). Alternatively, you can go almost directly north to the motorway through **Srednje**, Kladanj, and close to Tuzla.

The first is shorter, but slightly more strenuous because of its mountainous character and all its twists and turns. You reach flatter ground only at **Zvornik**, at the end of a long artificial lake that's part of the River Drina (see above). The second road's a little faster over the early stretch (and also extremely attractive), flattish around Tuzla, and flat again after a very hilly section beyond Tuzla. Both routes are decidedly scenic, though.

On the second one you go through the little town of **Kladanj,** a very prosperous spot today. Basically, it's a small mountain spa, one of scores in Yugoslavia (some still decidedly flourishing: Yugoslavs don't imagine pills are the answer to every ailment). One day someone jokingly told a passing German motorist that its

spring water restores male virility. The town now exports large quantities of bottled water.

Travnik, Jajce and Banja Luka

You reach all three of these towns by taking the Zagreb road out of Sarajevo. It by-passes Visoko and avoids going through Zenica, Yugoslavia's main steel town.

Travnik, our first worthwhile stop, is a pleasant spot, hememed in by mountains as virtually every Bosnian town is, but with more fertile slopes around than you see in many places. The town centre's mainly Turkish. There's a well-preserved old fortress on top of the hill immediately above it, with a Turkish burial ground on the hillside below.

The town was Nobel prizewinner Ivo Andrič's birthplace and contains a museum dedicated to him. There's a summer-and-winter resort at **Babanovac** on Mount Vlašić, 15 miles from Travnik. The region's noted for its broad mountain pastures. Babanovac has a ski-lift and ski-jump. Package holidays operate from UK.

Jajce provides the sort of romantic-old-town photograph that everyone loves. Its oldest part spreads up the slopes of a conical hill to a picturesque fortress on the top. Turkish houses, mosque minarets, and a typical church belltower all form part of the scene. The River Pliva flows at the foot of the hill on its way to join the nearby Vrbas. Upstream it forms a charmingly peaceful lake, ringed with woods and with a hotel beside it. Downstream it falls sharply in a series of spectacular waterfalls. The standard photograph shows both the waterfalls and the conical fortress-topped hill.

Inevitably, one feels, a Yugoslav spot as beautiful as this must have been the scene of bitter fighting. Jajce was certainly Bosnia's capital in the years immediately before the Turks took over. In WWII however it's remembered as the spot where the council that served as a provisional parliament – occupied Europe's only one, incidentally – decided the shape of the country's future government on the night of 29–30 November 1943. 29 November's celebrated by Yugoslavs worldwide as their national day.

To reach **Banja Luka** you take the road that drops quickly into the spectacular Vrbas gorge, not the one going out past the lake to Bihać, Karlovac, and Zagreb (Chapter 11). For the best part of 50 miles you travel in the bottom of a long, deep canyon, with woods on either side. Banja Luka marks the canyon's end. It's a very pleasant mixture of very old, mainly Turkish remains, with equally attractive modern housing and workplaces, all built around a large, ancient fortress standing on flat land beside the now quiet River Vrbas. Exploring the fortress is a cheering experience. It has been turned into a lovely park, which local youngsters enjoy to the full.

If you take the road northwest out of Banja Luka toward Prijedor you come to legendary **Mount Kozara**, yet another of Yugoslavia's National Parks. It's densely forested. But that's not the reason why, to Yugoslavs, it's almost holy ground. One of WWII's most terrible battles was fought here. A magnificent monument on one of the peaks, Mrakovica, commemorates nearly 10,000 Partisan troops who lost their lives here, along with over 35,000 civilians, including 11,000 children under 14, who were murdered by the Germans.

The earliest Protestants?

About 15 miles of narrow road lead southwest from Počitelj (Chapter 8). They bring you to **Radimlje**. If this little spot's included in an excursion – as it well may be – the purpose is to show you one of Bosnia's largest collection of stećci. They're gravestones – but of a very special sort. Some are carved, either with patterns or with scenes of everyday life. Most are large, and some are enormous. There's one weighing 14 tons at the entrance to the Bosnian National Museum in Sarajevo. Thousands are scattered over almost all Bosnia, though the groups at Radimlje and nearby **Stolac** are particularly impressive. None can be dated later than about 1200.

They belong to a Christian sect called the Bogomils. No one knows very much about them. But it's clear that they rebelled fiercely against existing church laws and administration. They maintained connections with the Cathares of southern France, and like the Cathares were savagely persecuted till their beliefs died out. Like the Cathares, and Czechoslovakia's later Hussites, who maintained good contact with English friends, their beliefs heralded the Protestant revolution that eventually swept much of Europe. But no one knows why there were so many of them in remote Bosnia, or what exactly their beliefs and reasoning were. All we have that's certain is their tombstones – and even then we don't know the significance of the different sorts of carving on them.

GENERAL INFORMATION

Chapter Seventeen

The Background to Your Visit

Early History

Our descriptions of Yugoslavia's various regions have inevitably included a good deal of history. One of the country's fascinations is the amount of the past that you can't help seeing on the ground. It ranges from striking prehistoric settlements to Roman buildings still in use, vast Byzantine fortresses and settlements, churches that go back almost to the beginnings of Christianity in both Western Europe and among the Slavs, magnificent medieval monasteries, superb Venice-inspired towns, fine Turkish towns and buildings, and traces of the other invaders who have attacked the region in the last 3000 years.

The Slavs were themelves invaders who settled in the 6th and 7th centuries and merged with indigenous tribes and Roman and other "foreigners". They themselves were then invaded by Byzantines, Bulgarians, Venetians, Hungarians, Tatars and other marauding tribes, Turks, and Austrians before South Slav (Yugo-slav) territory was merged into the Kingdom of Yugoslavia in 1918.

Even that brought little peace. The Italians were given Istria and seized much of the coast and islands. Politicians from the country's constituent areas fought bitterly among themselves. Croat–Serb rivalry was especially fierce. Government degenerated into an unsettled dictatorship dominated largely by foreign dictators and particularly by the Nazis.

What little history we're taught in Britain includes virtually nothing that happened east or north of Vienna. We find it difficult to understand why the Yugoslavs seem so obsessed with their centuries of foreign domination, and why Slobodan ("Free") became such a popular boy's first name after 1945 (girls tended to be called Mira – Peace). The fact is that it wasn't till 1945 that the South Slavs felt themselves masters of their own destiny. The unity that they'd fought for under long years of often excessively oppressive Turkish and Austro-Hungarian rule hadn't resulted in real self-rule, or even the unity that ordinary citizens wanted.

What finally united millions from all classes was an explicit 1941 pact signed by the Yugoslav government with Hitler and Mussolini.

Tito and the Partisans

The whole country exploded in spontaneous revolt, and was invaded by Italian, German, Hungarian, and Bulgarian armies. Two Serbian generals, Mihailović and Nedić, brought their troops out in patriotic opposition. The Nazis gave the Croatian nationalist quisling Pavelić his own army, the Ustaše, and complete control of Croatia. The 12,000 unarmed members of the outlawed Communist Party, under their General Secretary Josip Broz, codenamed Tito, used their existing power to organise coordinated nationwide resistance.

Pavelić and his Ustaše soon took to murdering Serbs, Jews, gipsies, Croat opponents and, of course, communist supporters. Mihailović and the Četniks, as his army was called, soon proved keener on killing fellow Yugoslavs – particularly Croatians, Muslims, and Communists – than on fighting the national enemy. His obsession was restoring the Serbian monarchy. Before long he was actively cooperating with the Axis forces. Nedić's and the non-Axis invaders' efforts tended to peter out. But not before huge damage had been done.

Tito and his Partisans, as they became called, made steady progress, even though most of their arms had at first to be stolen from their enemies. In November 1942 they held the first meeting of occupied Europe's only free parliament. In November 1943, despite the lies put about by Mihailović's well-connected supporters and the Yugoslav royal government-in-exile in London (and repeated even by the BBC), help from the Western Allies was added to small quantities of help getting through from the USSR. Brigadier Sir Fitzroy Maclean (as he now is) was seconded from the Foreign Office and parachuted to join Tito as head of a British military mission. In the terrible campaigns that followed he became one of Tito's closest friends.

Tito collected some remarkable helpers around himself. They included the sons and daughters of several men who were his bitterest enemies (a judge who had sent him to prison, a leading government-in-exile minister, the man who had outlawed the Communist Party, etc), and also the former schoolmaster Kardelj. Considerable Partisan effort went into education, even during their desperate fighting.

Though 8000 of the original 12,000 Communist Party members were killed in battle, by 1945 the Partisans had four armies totalling 800,000 men (and some women) in the field. By May they had cleared the invaders from all Yugoslav territory. On 29 November 1945 the modern country's first Constitution was promulgated. The Yugoslavs were at last free of centuries of hated foreign domination.

The problems of peace

The country was in a desperate condition. Of its original 15-million population 1.7 million had been killed, over 500,000 by fellow-Yugoslavs. What little industry had once existed was in ruins. On the railways only 16 locomotives were still working, most bridges had been dynamited, and long stretches of line destroyed. Hundreds of villages had been burned, and their inhabitants shot. One survivor in four was homeless. Groups of starving orphans were roaming the countryside. Worst of all, political battles were still raging.

Mihailović was captured and executed. Nedić committed suicide. But Četniks and others who escaped to the West continued their political campaigns and intrigues – and still continue them today. It's difficult to envisage the fanatical fury that still drags on unless you or your friends have been involved.

The last decade has seen several murders of Yugoslavs by fellow Yugoslavs in Western Europe. Any Yugoslav coming to live in the West, for whatever reason, is liable to be badgered to support anti-Tito propaganda and activities. Because British troops in Austria in 1945 returned Yugoslavs accused of war crimes to Yugoslavia Macmillan, then Prime Minister, has himself been accused of war crimes by a leading Young Conservative. A libel action is actually now in progress because of similar accusations against a British general.

Anti-Partisan factions in the West still maintain the stranglehold on the Western press which enabled them to induce the wartime BBC and all the lesser media to lie. They've successfully prevented any attempt to report fairly – except to some extent by the Financial Times.

A unique way of life

The fact which all this too-readily-believed propaganda obscures is that the Yugoslavs, since about 1953, have been developing a completely new system of political, social, and economic organisation, totally unlike anything ever attempted anywhere else. One difficulty about understanding it is that its concepts are all new and therefore require new words to denote them. But you can't grasp the new concepts till you understand the terms, and you don't understand the new terms till you've grasped the new concepts.

However, the basic idea is that no one should allow other people to run his/her life. You don't elect other people to make your decisions. You do it yourself. One in five of the entire voting population is at any moment actively involved in decision-making. Tenure of major offices is very limited – Prime Minister 4 years (and only once in a lifetime), trade union regional chairman 1 year, and so on.

As far as possible what we consider the normal government bodies – local (commune) councils, Republic assemblies, and the Federal assembly – have very restricted powers. The Federal Assembly, for instance, manages the police, the fulltime defence forces, the diplomatic service, certain nationally collected taxes such as Customs duties, and surprisingly little else, apart from coordinating decisions made by the various Republics' assemblies. It's having terrible difficulty as this is being written in devising a nationally acceptable economic policy to cope with the country's (and the world's) current severe economic problems. It has no real method of enforcement.

The system's immensely complicated, and we can't begin to describe it here. But let's take some relatively simple examples.

Yugoslavia's national health service is based directly on the UK's. But no government body – not even the communes – has a finger in running it. It's run by taxpayers and health service workers combined.

Health care deductions from salaries are paid direct to each commune's health board (roughly 520 communes make up the whole country). Each health board is composed equally of delegates representing all grades of health workers and delegates representing the taxpayers (who are also, of course, patients). "Delegates" in Yugoslav terminology aren't people who invent their own policies. Their job's to keep their electors fully informed and to voice their electors' views. They can be recalled if they fail in this. And they can never represent the same electors for more than two 4-year terms. All public services, such as education, welfare, pensions, etc, are run like this.

Commercial concerns, from road-cleaning to atomic power, are controlled by the people who work in them. Everyone joining a "work organisation" (company to us) does so on an individually-written contractual basis that gives him/her equal status with everyone else in the same organisation. The workers elect a "workers council" with all the powers (and more) of a Western board of directors. No one can be sacked except by his/her fellow-workers on the workers council, and the law demands that sacking should be avoided if humanly possible.

Even new technology doesn't result in automatic redundancies. First, people are offered retraining. If they can't cope with that they're found simpler jobs or help with finding work elsewhere. In the last resort the older ones will be offered early retirement on favourable terms. Unemployment in Yugoslavia is high. But once you've got a job it's pretty difficult to lose it.

Workplaces and their equipment belong to everyone – not to any identifiable shareholders and least of all to the State, specifically precluded by the Constitution from any

commercial activity. People using the workplace and its installations fix their own salaries within parameters agreed between the powerful trade unions and the trade associations inside each branch of activity. They're legally obliged to run their concerns for the community's as well as their own good. Profit isn't the overpowering motive it is in the West.

It's an amazingly complex system. Because it's totally new it's not easy to operate. It's evolving all the time. Problems that emerge are constantly monitored and corrected. But the DIY principles that we've outlined permeate everything.

Should hostilities occur, for instance, the entire population automatically becomes part of the country's defence forces – and everyone's trained in what he or she should do. All the larger workplaces even have their own armouries and workers trained to use the weapons. Women provide support services.

Schools are run by "workers councils" that include pupil delegates, and hospitals (there are no GPs of our type) by workers councils that include all grades from top consultants to porters and cleaners.

Merely describing the system's aims, quite apart from its problems and evolution, would require a fat volume. It's significant of the West's extraordinary refusal even to look that only two serious partial descriptions have ever been published here – both by the United Nations' International Labour Office based in Geneva (*Workers' Management in Yugoslavia*, 1982, and *The Trade Union Situation and Industrial Relations in Yugoslavia*, 1985). They're available in English from ILO's London office.

Tourism

But how does all this affect holidaymakers? In general, very little. The bulk of visitors are still persuaded by their media that the State runs everything in Yugoslavia. In fact it runs nothing.

The one result of all these innovations that you're likely to come across has been christened the "surly waiter syndrome". If a waiter or waitress or anyone else feels offended or upset there's little to stop him behaving in a bad-tempered way.

It's no use complaining to the hotel manager. You may think he's the boss, but he's actually the workers council's employee, far more likely to be dispensed with at the end of his renewable 4-year contract than any ordinary employee. So, if you feel something's really wrong, content yourself with having a quiet word to your tour operator's rep. With luck, he or she will find out what's wrong and sort it out.

The need to do this is happily pretty rare. For the most part you'll find the Yugoslavs extremely friendly and helpful – provided, of course, that you don't throw your weight about and make yourself even unintentionally troublesome.

It may be worth bearing in mind that tourism in Yugoslavia began seriously only in the mid- to late-1960s, and is only now beginning to run on a really sound basis. It's slowly being extended to inland areas from the coast.

One feature of tourism throws fascinating light on Yugoslav attitudes. Toplessness on beaches isn't so much either frowned on or encouraged as just not noticed. You can do what you like. There are a large number of naturist beaches to which everyone is now admitted (previously you had to be a member of a naturist organisation).

Women, in their work and in public life, are completely equal with men in Yugoslavia. The old habits of male domination are still much in evidence at home however.

Meeting the Yugoslavs

Because of language difficulties and Yugoslavs' sensitivities about their own poverty compared with the Western world it's not easy to get to know Yugoslavs well enough to be invited into their homes and allowed to live on the same level as your hosts. As a stranger, your best chance is by taking private-house accommodation in inland towns. Once you've become really friendly you'll find the Yugoslavs almost embarrassingly kind and hospitable.

People you meet during ordinary travel can sometimes seem maddeningly laid back. They're totally free of our Western obsessions with hurrying. If you're on holiday, why do you want to rush about anyway? If a meal takes a long time to serve you're more likely to speed it up by explaining carefully that you've a boat to catch in half an hour than by shouting.

Policemen, and some other officials, on the other hand, often seem to be convinced that foreign visitors must be made to toe the line very strictly, whatever their fellow-Yugoslavs may do. You may find yourself forbidden to park except in an empty parking-space while Yugoslavs are double-banked a few yards away. You may be forced to keep to the path while a dozen Yugoslavs in front of you walk across the grass. Just grin and put up with it.

127

One thing worth bearing in mind is that Yugoslavs' incomes are only a tiny fraction of ours. Average earnings are about £1200 a year ($2000). Professional people and managers are paid on the same level. The Prime Minister's salary, for instance, is fixed at 4 times the average wage – rather less than a typist gets in UK. Money admittedly goes further – but not that much. When you realise this it puts the extraordinary generosity you come across in the country in a very different perspective.

Music and the arts

We've seen a good deal of Yugoslavia's enormously varied architecture while travelling round the country. It's a subject worth studying by itself. A lot of modern work is also worth a good look. Some of the earlier coastal hotels may be less than exciting. But many towns, small as well as large, have been made very attractive. Architects, like all Yugoslavs, are extremely independent-minded. What many are trying to do is to design buildings that *aren't* aping the fashions popular elsewhere.

In art the country has much more to offer than is generally realised in the West. There are far more good sculptors than just Meštrović, as you'll realise if you look at just a few of the main war memorials. With us, these look mostly as though they're glorifying war. The Yugoslavs all know what misery war brings, and monuments like those in Ljubljana, on Mount Kozara, at Tjentište and elsewhere are beautiful expressions of the horror they feel.

Much the same applies to painting. The best-known modern works are those of the "naive" peasant painters from Hlebine and elsewhere. But there's a good deal else that's well worth seeing.

Yugoslavia possesses some of the world's best cartoonists and animated film-makers. They've produced a number of very striking straight films, too, though they've not been aimed primarily at big-money markets which Yugoslavs are anyway out of tune with. Their theatre productions can also be very good indeed.

In music their strengths are equally divided between traditional (village "folk") and classical. Traditional music's specially fascinating because it reflects the country's hugely-varied cultures. In Bosnia and Macedonia it's largely Turkish-based. In Dalmatia the extraordinary village "ganga" singing can be paralleled in parts of Albania, in Bulgaria, and in pockets all the way to the Caucasus and beyond. Dalmatian urban singing by local "klape", on the other hand, is based on West European harmonies introduced mainly by Austrian 19th century musician visitors.

Real "oral-composition" epic ballad singing has died out. But in Dalmatia and Serbia and Montenegro and elsewhere you can still hear ballads whose texts have become "frozen" (as Homer was by the 6th century BC and Beowulf over 1000 years later). And they're still accompanied by the amazingly resonant one-stringed gusla, played by the singer. Lots of other traditional instruments are also still in use. Folklore performances put on for tourists are of a much higher and much more authentic standard than in many countries.

Orthodox chant, whose roots go back to ancient Greek music, also deserves mention. It can be exceptionally beautiful. Unfortunately very few Western musicians have the least understanding or knowledge of it.

Not many Yugoslav "classical" composers have become well known in the West. Matičić, Mokranjac, and Skerjanc are among the names known and respected by Western professionals.

As with music, the country's visual folk art flourishes and is excellent. Carpets, brassware, embroideries, woodcarving, and much else is well worth having. Books, too, are often extremely well printed. Colour work, in particular, can be outstanding and surprisingly cheap.

In literature we've mentioned Ivo Andrić, who won the Nobel prize in 1961. Apart from him not many Yugoslav authors are at all well known in the West. It is, however, a very literary country, with an astonishing output of books, newspapers, and magazines. Printing's cheap, and self-publishing's common. Because the Constitution precludes the State from undertaking any commercial activity official publications intended for sale are produced by independent publishers.

Food and drink

Food Yugoslavia can't boast much in the way of fine cooking. But the food that the Yugoslavs themselves prefer is excellently wholesome – superb plain grills, *pršut* (= Italian prosciutto – stringy Parma-style smoked ham), *cevapčiči* (grilled minced lamb in finger-length rolls, sprinkled with chopped raw onion), *ražnjiči* (kebabs), *brodet* (fish stew), *djuvec* (Serbian casserole of meat, aubergine, and rice – there's also a Bosnian casserole totally indistinguishable from Lancashire hotpot), *sarma* (minced meat and rice wrapped in vine or cabbage leaves), stuffed peppers, *musaka* similar to the Greek dish but not necessarily including potatoes, together with home-produced sauerkraut (exported to many countries), a fair choice of Turkish-style sugar pastries (*blini*, *kadaif*, etc), and sheep's or mixed sheep's and cow's milk cheeses such as *kačkaval* or *Pagski sir* (cheese from Pag island). A refreshing cold fruit soup is sometimes also served in the better Dalmatian hotels.

Unfortunately, most hotel restaurants persist with "international" dishes such as spaghetti bolognese and the like. So try one of the small family-run restaurants if you can. They're usually (but not invariably) located at the edges of resorts and are easily distinguishable by their mass of noisily cheerful Yugoslav customers.

Prices are modest – except for slabs of newly-grilled lamb and for fish dishes. You can eat well for about £3.50 if you steer clear of these dishes and of obvious tourist-trap restaurants (reckon £4.50–£5 in these). Self-service bars are even cheaper and usually extremely good value.

Why restaurants should charge so much for fish is a mystery. Magnificent fresh fish and shellfish costs practically nothing in the early-morning markets. It's something you just have to accept. Make an effort to buy fresh seafood for your self-catering meals (which may mean a very early trek to town or the quayside).

Drinks Table wines are good and cheap. Vintages are only just beginning to be distinguished, but there are a number of distinctive wine regions, especially in Dalmatia. Much of Slovenia's production's sold abroad.

Plavac (*plav* means blue and the wine's a very dark red–blue in colour) comes from the Pelješac peninsula, as does the heavy red *Dingač*. Light white *Grk*, meaning "Greek", is produced along the coast. *Žilavka* is made from the žilavka grape, one of the very few varieties that escaped Europe's devastating phylloxera epidemic in 1866. But the only really good Žilavka comes from the tiny Blagaj area just outside Sarajevo, where the vine survived. *Maraština* is a pleasant dessert wine. But this is a tiny part of your choice. Local wines exist everywhere.

Šlivovica plum brandy is the national firewater. You gulp it in small glassfuls like vodka. It's tremendous once you've got the taste. *Rakija* can mean šlivovica or any one of several strong drinks. *Lozovača* contains plentiful herbs in brandy and belongs to Dalmatia. *Komovica* isn't dissimilar. *Vinjak* resembles a sort of cross between very heavy wine and brandy. Many Yugoslavs drink nothing else, but some visitors hate it.

Maraschino, which we use to preserve cherries or pour over desserts (and occasionally drink neat), was invented at the Maraska Distillery in Zadar when the town was part of Italy. Some years ago Maraska invented a superb apéritif which they named (in English) Half and Half. It's vastly better than most bitters, but sales never seem to extend more than about ten miles from Zadar (the locals know a good thing when they've got it). If you can't get Half and Half (as will happen unless you're in Zadar) buy *Istra Bitter*, the next best thing. Bought in ordinary shops a bottle should cost little more than £1 or $2. It's useful for duty free purchases, especially if you think you can persuade your home Customs that it's just a wine.

In Yugoslav airport duty-free shops the wines are incidentally ridiculously expensive. Patronise ordinary grocers before departure.

Further reading

Very few UK or US publications fill out effectively the various aspects of Yugoslavia dealt with here. For general descriptions of towns and countryside your best bet is the numerous English-language coffee-table productions of Yugoslav publishers such as Yugoslav Review (Terazije 31, 11000 Belgrade) and Yugoslaviapublic, Knez Mihailova 10, 11000 Belgrade. Their photographs are invariably excellent. Texts are normally written by experts and well translated. Printing can be excellent. Write for lists of books in print and payment methods.

Yugoslaviapublic's *Treasures of Yugoslavia: An encyclopedic touring guide* is outstanding. It's massively illustrated with superbly printed colour photographs. Its very detailed maps are also excellent.

On the subject of the country's present political system, we've already mentioned the two books published by the International Labour Office, Geneva. They stand alone. Many historical accounts are either very tendentious or plain rubbish. Fitzroy Maclean however has written effectively about wartime events in his *Eastern Approaches*. Professor Phyllis Auty, formerly of the London University School of Slavonic and East European studies, has produced a number of sound general accounts. In 1946 she did a major report on Yugoslavia's desperate position for Picture Post. It was a very strenuous job.

Your public library will have copies of

these works, and also of translations of many books by the Nobel prizewinner Ivo Andrić.

One of the Yugoslav Review publications you may find specially enlightening is *Yugoslav Story*, by the Time-Life war correspondent/photographer John Phillips. His account of wartime experiences with the Partisans, and of later visits to Yugoslavia, is backed up by scores of superb photographs. He interviewed and photographed Mihailović in his cell during the trial.

Yugoslav National Tourist Offices can produce material dealing with everything of tourist interest. Embassies have information about art, theatre, etc in Yugoslavia, and also English-language versions of all sorts of documents, such as the current Constitution, the main laws, up-to-date reports by bodies investigating what's going wrong in the country, and so on. They're very enlightening once you know what all their strange technical jargon means, but not much use till then. The International Labour Office volumes attempt partial glossaries. But not very successfully.

While you're in Yugoslavia you should be able to pick up little local guides that are often detailed and scholarly. Bookshops in major resorts such as Dubrovnik may also stock good coffee-table books by the two publishers mentioned above and the many others with shorter lists and more specialised interests. Do have a look at them.

Chapter Eighteen

Practical Information

Before you leave

You can travel to Yugoslavia on a British Visitor's Passport, valid 1 year, as well as on a full passport, valid 10 years. Application forms for both, with full instructions, are available at main post offices. Apply in very good time. You can stay for up to 3 months without a visa.

Carry your main money in the form of traveller's cheques (which will be replaced immediately if lost or stolen). You may be able to buy Yugoslav dinars at favourable rates before departure. But you can't import (or export) more than 5000, and only in notes of 1000 and below. To avoid starting home with illegal sums take some traveller's cheques in small denominations and/or make certain you've a few £5 notes (or small dollar bills) to change for final small purchases. In theory you can exchange surplus dinars at the airport. But it isn't always easy. Main credit cards can be used if necessary at the larger hotels, airline offices, etc.

Take your driving licence if you're liable to use a car. Also log book and green card insurance if you're taking your own car. Sports boats can be imported for indefinite periods without a licence.

Stock up with personal items you or your children are likely to need – toiletries, films, sun cream, medicines, nappies, babyfoods, sunglasses and so on. They may – or may not – be available at your resort. Independent travellers going off the beaten track should also take soap.

If travelling independently, get all the information you can from the Yugoslav National Tourist Office in London or New York about long-distance bus and train connections, big-town tourist office addresses, and so on. Mull it over carefully in advance. For things like wildlife photographic tours in National Parks you may have to write/phone regional tourist offices in Yugoslavia. London or New York will give you addresses and phone numbers. But start asking for information months in advance.

If you book flight-only tickets to a charter-only airport such as Pula or Krk find out how to get into town from the airport. There may be no public buses, only relatively expensive taxis.

If you like to take duty-free Scotch or gin with you it may be as well to know that you're strictly allowed to import only half a litre into Yugoslavia. But no Yugoslav Customs officer has ever been known to question drink imports.

After you arrive

INFORMATION If you've bought a package from a reputable tour operator the firm's reps will have all the information you're likely to need, or will know where to get it.

If you're travelling independently you can consult "tourist offices" in most towns. To a large extent however these are fundamentally commercial concerns, more interested in selling you excursions or private house accommodation and so on than in just answering questions. Though most help as much as they can, efficiency varies. The big travel firms (Putnik, Atlas, Kompas, Dalmacijaturist, and the rest) have offices in all main centres, and sometimes handle private-house bookings. In the big inland towns this may be looked after by offices that aren't always easy to find. Get addresses in advance.

PASSPORTS Don't be alarmed if your hotel or campsite takes your passport for 24 hours or so on arrival. You'll be given a receipt you can show the police if necessary. You're supposed to carry your passport at all times (well, if you're going further than the beach) – even if you're scudding around the open sea in an outboard dinghy wearing nothing but a swimsuit. But the police don't hassle you in resort areas.

EXCHANGING MONEY You'll get exactly the same rate at all exchange offices. The central government handles all foreign currency exchange (one of its relatively few powers). Hotel exchange desks open only part-time. Note opening times when you arrive.

GETTING AROUND Bus stations in all main towns sell tickets for all services passing through the town. Also seat reservations for services originating there. In the larger ones you'll have to go to the right window.

Consult the destination board. Choose your departure time, and go to the right company's window. In case of language problems write down in large, clear letters the number of tickets you want (1 x, or 3 x, or whatever), your destination, the date you want to travel (in figures in the British, not the American order – 2.12.88 = 2 December 1988, not 12 February; or use the normal English abbreviation for the month – Aug, Sept, etc), and the departure time in 24-hour notation (19.30 = 7.30 pm).

Once on the bus, remember that your seat number is on the back of your seat, not facing you on the back of the one in front. Don't expect the air conditioning to work: be grateful when it does. And be wary of upsetting fellow passengers by insisting on opening windows. On long journeys there's time to buy ice creams, soft drinks, snacks, etc at intermediate stops.

You can sometimes buy local town-service bus tickets from tobacconists etc or hotel receptionists. Otherwise from the driver. There's a fixed charge for all town-service rides.

Larger **railway** stations tend to have ticket clerks with at least a few words of English or German. Again, problems can be forestalled by putting down on paper the number of tickets you want, your destination, and the departure time of the train you plan to catch. There are no reductions for returns. If you want to buy a return ticket with seat reservations put that down too.

InterRail and Eurail are valid in Yugoslavia. So are Rail Europ senior citizen cards, available to British Rail senior citizen cardholders. The reductions are worthwhile even on Yugoslav Railways' minuscule fares.

Avoid local services on near-derelict rolling stock.

Good, modern sleepers and couchettes are available on the longer "Inter-City" trains (the English term's used and a small supplement charged). Sleepers cost only about £5 or £6 per person (US$9–11). Full meals are also available on many long journeys at extremely reasonable prices – £6–£7 (US$11–13) for two, including a bottle of very drinkable wine. Children under 12 pay half fare.

Getting travel information for cross-country rail journeys can pose problems. Ticket clerks and even enquiry office staff in smaller centres seem to have little experience of extracting details from timetables. Try to find a friendly English-speaking Yugoslav with experience of travel to interpret for you, preferably someone who studies the route map first and knows where connections can be made.

Plane tickets for domestic routes can be bought at main travel agents as well as airline offices and airports. Prices are low, provided you book inside Yugoslavia, not in your own country.

Taxis can be found in every place of any size. Except in main coast resorts charges are low.

WHERE TO STAY? If buying a package your travel agent should be able to get all the hotel details you want from any good tour operator. If travelling on your own remember that, in coast resorts, only the most expensive hotels cater for independent travellers, and even those usually have mostly group bookings. Individuals can find themselves a bit overlooked. Inland, things are different. Prices for foreigners aren't low: Yugoslavs and East Europeans pay a different rate.

This was avoided for many years, but proved inescapable in the end.

You can always ask a tourist office to find rooms for you. The pleasantest non-package places to stay can be the smaller guesthouses (the Yugoslavs use their phonetic transliteration of the French word *pansioni* for them). Food and rooms are usually both good, and inexpensive. Genuine private-house rooms (without food) can be had for up to about US$10 a night (sometimes less) in most resorts and inland towns. On the coast, rooms let to foreigners are usually on the upper floors of modern, custom-built concrete-built houses where the family occupies the ground floor. Accommodation prices drop steeply outside the high season.

If you plan to use Youth Hostels the International Handbook provides full information. There are enough hostels to make touring the whole country possible.

Campsites vary enormously in quality and cleanliness. Advance reservations aren't possible. You just have to find one you like. The best are very good indeed. They often occupy lovely sites and have extemely helpful staff.

Self-catering accommodation is all modern and usually very well planned and located.

ELECTRICITY 220 volts, 60 cycles. Two-pin plugs, rather similar to the USA's are used. Multiple adaptors usually fit.

RESTAURANTS, BARS, AND CAFÉS Hotel restaurants mostly look after you well. You occasionally come across the "surly waiter syndrome" – a waiter (or waitress) who's fed up, or whom you've unintentionally upset. Don't lose your temper (see Chapter 17). The Yugoslav system allows virtually no way of "disciplining" the waiter (see Chapter 17). If trouble continues, have a word to your rep, who may know or be able to discover what's causing the trouble.

When you go out to eat you'll find the larger resorts have a fair range of obviously touristy places where English is spoken and where prices may be relatively high – a menu can usually be inspected at the entrance. Be a bit more adventurous and find a place full of Yugoslavs. It's a sure sign that the food's good. These are often family-run, and everyone knows that to keep the customers arriving they've got to keep them happy.

There's no shortage of bars and cafés. Most open at 7 or 8 am and close at 11 or 12 pm. Café ice creams and pastries are often delicious, and you usually have a choice of expresso or tiny cups of strong, black, thick Turkish coffee (Turkska kava). *Aficionados* chew the dregs. Yugoslav drinking law is simple. It's expressed in notices saying: "We do not serve alcoholic drinks before 8 am" (7 am in summer, the time when most factories and offices start work).

TIPPING Except for taxi drivers, not essential unless special help or specially good service has been provided – though it's becoming normal in tourist hotels and restaurants. Taxi drivers, as everywhere, expect a bit extra. Ten per cent is ample. Baggage porters, where they exist, have fixed charges.

SHOPS AND MARKETS If you choose self-catering you can buy everything you need at a supermarket – though the open-air markets are cheaper for fresh fruit and vegetables,

and more fun. Souvenirs, such as carved wooden bowls, Turkish-style brassware, wall carpets, Kelim rugs, embroidered blouses and skirts, and other craft products are sold everywhere. Good duty-free shops, where you use Western currency, exist in many resorts.

If you're interested in things like coffee-table books or men's suits you may find some bargains. Prices of existing products aren't raised to match galloping inflation. So you may pick up, say, a well-made light summer suit in a main shopping-centre that would be a bargain at its normal price of £40–£50 (US$75–90) for a mere £10–11 (say, $20). Or a £35 magnificently printed and bound illustrated coffee-table book (the colour-printing is usually superb) for a mere £5. Some shops give a 10% reduction for payment in foreign currency (which can be banked separately and carries certain privileges).

PRICES Prices in general are much lower than in Western countries. Because of Yugoslavia's galloping inflation it's impossible to quote exact rates. Ordinary Yugoslavs suffer appallingly because of inflation. Foreigners don't, because exchange rates keep pace.

OPENING HOURS From May to October shops usually open 08.00–12.00 and 17.00–20.00; 09.00–14.00 the rest of the year – though resort hours can be much longer. Most offices open at 07.00 or 08.00 and close not later than 14.30 – banks at 12.00. Government offices work mostly 07.00–15.00 Some large supermarkets and department stores stay open all day: the term for all-day opening is "non-stop". Many shops close early on Saturday (except in resorts).

PUBLIC HOLIDAYS The following are national holidays: 1 April, Good Friday, Easter Monday, 1 May, 27 May, 4 July, 27 August, 29–30 November. If any falls on a Sunday the following Monday becomes a holiday. Each Republic celebrates also its own Uprising Day in commemoration of the 1941 revolt – Slovenia 22 July, Croatia 27 July, Serbia 7 July, Macedonia 2 August and 11 October, Bosnia–Hercegovina 27 July.

Sports and entertainment Many hotels nowadays have swimming pools. Pleasant sunbathing may be possible in a garden setting. Sandy beaches are scarce (see Chapter 2); stretches of fine gravel exist, but you often swim from rocks that have cemented areas for sunbathing. Beach umbrellas and deck chairs can usually be hired. Surfboards are normally available, with instruction if you need it. You find tennis courts in a number of places, and one or two resorts offering "family" holidays provide all sorts of facilities for youngsters. See our resort descriptions and consult your travel agent/tour operator. If you want to ride at Lipice you'll have to bring jodhpurs and boots. Bled possesses Yugoslavia's only golf course. Equipment can be hired at ski resorts used by foreign holidaymakers.

Every resort hotel has some sort of nightspot or bar where music of some sort is provided in the evenings, and many have discos too. Sophisticated nightclubs are rare. Displays of local traditional music and dance are common, and are usually good. Casinos exist only in major resorts and big cities. Admission is limited to foreigners and employees (take your passport) and you have to use Western currencies (take your traveller's cheques).

Many coast resorts hold festivals of various sorts in July or July and August. Those at Split and Dubrovnik include theatre and music of all sorts. Opatija (July only) runs to opera and ballet as well. You can get married at the Ljubljana "Peasant Wedding" in May, or at Bohinj's similar mass-splicing spree in July. Pula holds a film festival in the Roman amphitheatre every July–August, and spectacular horse-riding and tilting can be seen at Sinj (inland from Split) in July, and also at Požarevac (Serbia) in September. More specialised events include Varaždin's October Puppet Theatre Festival, and Belgrade's international BITEF Theatre Festival in September (with chamber theatres coming together in April). Half the world's animated films are screened in Zagreb in June. And, of course, there are Zagreb's two annual trade fairs.

If you want to know about specialised activities, such as sailing, canoeing, fishing, and also about the country's numerous still-flourishing spas you can get virtually all the information you're likely to need from a National Tourist Office. We've given some indications. But lack of space makes it impossible to deal fully with these topics.

PHOTOGRAPHY You can photograph anything you like except defence installations and troops in formation. Market stallholders are used to being continuously photographed by tourists (very colourful they are, too!). But it's courteous to indicate that you'd like to photograph people, and give them the chance to refuse. They're usually delighted to help.

WILDLIFE Yugoslavia places a high value on conservation and care of the countryside. The Plitvice, Kornati, and Durmitor National Parks are particularly worth visiting, as indeed are the others mentioned in our text. Far more bird sanctuaries and nature reserves exist than we've talked about here. Yugoslav National Tourist Offices however can put you in touch with specialist wildlife and birdwatching societies and the like. Good hunting (wild boar, mouflon, etc) is also available in several areas.

CHILDREN They're always made very welcome, though there aren't always many special facilities for them. The best bets are the places that advertise "family" holidays (consult your travel agent/tour operator).

PROBLEMS AND EMERGENCIES

Whatever the difficulty, a reputable tour operator's rep should be able to sort it out. This includes things that go wrong with the hotel or apartment. They'll help too with things like collecting up essential receipts and the like for claims you may have to make against your insurance company.

Major tour operators' reps will also do what they can to help if you book flight-only travel with them. If you plan to wander round the country on your own, however, consider seriously a policy with someone like Europ Assistance. One phone call to London and they get their agents to look after everything, including paying the bills, getting you into hospital locally if that's considered advisable, and flying you straight home, by private ambulance plane if necessary, if that's thought preferable.

MOTORING Drivers of foreign-registered cars can use foreign currency at all frontier crossings to buy petrol coupons with a face value 10% above what you pay for them. Petrol stations are frequent, and nearly a hundred at key points sell lead-free petrol (ask for free map). Minor repairs are quickly and efficiently (and cheaply) dealt with – Yugoslav mechanics are masters of improvisation. For spares you'll have to rely on your insurance company – or make an excursion to Trieste (Trst to Yugoslavs), where stockists scattered all over the town sell spares for virtually all the world's cars.

In 1939 Yugoslavia had a total of less than 30 miles of surfaced road – including the towns. Today, major roads are nearly all excellent, though you'll find potholes on some less important routes. Only really out-of-the-way spots are still served by unsurfaced roads. Modern motorways are being constantly extended. In particular, the vital Ljubljana–Zagreb–Belgrade M1 stretch replacing the Germans' hastily-laid concrete wartime strip (which started breaking up within a few years) will be complete by the end of 1988. Its continuation to the Greek border at Gevgelija is already largely finished.

Signposting is mostly good. Driving isn't – unless there happens to be a policeman in sight, when it improves astonishingly. Police levy on-the-spot fines for speeding (they specialise in radar traps), wrong parking, etc.

Remember that it's forbidden to park actually on any out-of-town roadway. Pull off the road if you want to stop and, though it's not compulsory, put out warning triangles if you break down. Dialling 987 anywhere brings help (English-speakers will take your call in all major tourist areas, but give your location, etc slowly and clearly; start by saying very deliberately "Good morning/afternoon/evening" to establish that you're going to speak in English).

Yellow-painted AMSJ vans (Yugoslav Automobile Association) patrol tourist-frequented main roads and provide roadside help (at standard rates) and free advice.

Maps Yugoslav National Tourist Offices provide excellent free road maps giving up-to-date information about road surfaces. Further detail is available on the much larger Michelin 991.

Chapter Nineteen

A Look at the Language(s)

Yugoslavia's official language is Serbo-Croat (Srpski–Hvratski). It's an artificial mixture of Serbian and Croatian, sometimes called Croat–Serb (Hrvatski–Srpski) in Croatia. Serbian is spoken in Montenegro and Bosnia-Herzegovina, with local variations. Macedonia varies somewhat from both Serbian and Croatian, though not enough for Macedonians, Serbians, and Croatians to have serious difficulties understanding each other (ezero = lake in Macedonian = jezero elsewhere). Slovenian however is so different that other Yugoslavs may not understand it.

Pronunciation isn't difficult. Words are pronounced exactly as spelled and written exactly as pronounced. Stress-accents tend to come as early as possible in each word. Foreigners call Sarajevo Sarra-YAY-vo. Non-Bosnian Yugoslavs often pronounce it Sar-RAR-yay-vo. The locals tend to say SAR-a-ye-vo or SAR-'ye-vo. Dubrovnik has the stress on its first syllable – DOO-brov-nik.

The trouble about writing words exactly as pronounced is that different people pronounce the same word differently. So roadside signs wishing you SRETAN PUT and SREĆAN PUT both mean "bon voyage" (literally "lucky journey"). Krute and Kruta are both the same Dalmatian village (like the Lipice–Lipica spellings of the famous stud). But the stranger who thinks Kruče's the same place gets a shock when he finds it's a different spot several miles away.

The alphabets

Modified Roman alphabets are used in most of Yugoslavia and on all main road signs everywhere. Their use is increasing even where Cyrillic is still normal.

Q, W, X, and Y don't appear in Yugoslav Roman alphabets. B, D, F, K, L, M, N, P, S, T, V, and Z are pronounced as in English.

A sounds between cap and carp; C is prounounced as ts; Č as in church; Ć (not used in Slovenian) like the ty sound in nature when you're speaking pedantically; Dž, Dj, and Đ or đ all sound rather like the dg in edge, as does a G before E in Macedonian (eg, the town Gevgelija); G is otherwise "hard", as in egg; H is guttural, almost like K; I sounds as in pin or machine; J is equivalent to our consonantal Y (yet); O sounds between mop, mope, and more; R is strongly rolled and can be a vowel; Š is pronounced as sh in shall; U is like oo in good or fool (short or long); and Ž sounds like the s in pleasure.

All vowels are pronounced separately, except for -aj, -ej, and -oj, roughly equivalent to aye, main, and toy.

A Cyrillic alphabet is still standard in Bosnia, Macedonia, Montenegro, and

139

Serbia (eg, on railway stations and other public name-boards). It's not the same as either the Russian or Bulgarian alphabets. It was developed specially for the Yugoslav languages by Vuk Karadžić (1787–1864), the great Serbian writer, linguist, and ethnographer, whose work was a prime factor in encouraging the South Slav independence movement. Here's his alphabet, still in use, with its Yugoslav–Roman equivalents. Note the different letter order, based on the ancient Greek, from which Cyrillic's derived.

А	а	A	a
Б	б	B	b
В	в	V	v
Г	г	G	g
Д	д	D	d
Ђ	ђ	Dj	dj
Е	е	E	e
Ж	ж	Ž	ž
З	з	Z	z
И	и	I	i
J	j	Y	y
К	к	K	k
Љ	љ	L	l
Л	л	Lj	lj
М	м	M	m
Н	н	N	n
Њ	њ	Nj	nj
О	о	O	o
П	п	P	p
Р	р	R	r
С	с	S	s
Т	т	T	t
Ћ	ћ	Ć	ć
У	у	U	u
Ф	ф	F	f
Х	х	H	h
Ц	ц	C	c
Ч	ч	Č	č
Џ	џ	Dž	dž
Ш	ш	Š	š

Note that dj, đ, dž and, in Macedonian, g before e have near-identical sounds.

Remember, too, that in the Yugoslav Roman alphabets đ dj, dž, lj, and nj are regarded as single letters/sounds (following d, l, and n in lists). Đ follows D.

Some words and phrases (Croatian forms)

Sir!	Gospodine!
Madam!	Gospodjo!
Miss!	Gospodjice!
Please! Excuse me!	Molim!
Good day	Dobar dan
Good morning	Dobro jutro
Good evening	Dobar večer
Good night	Laku noć
How much?	Koliko?
Where?	Gdje?
When?	Kada?
When? (= At what time?)	U koliko sati?
Which?	Koji?
This (pronoun)	Ovo
That (pronoun)	Ono
No	Ne
Yes	Da
Thanks (very much)	Hvala (ljepo)
(To ask a question)	(Da) li . . . ?

    (eg, Ima sira = There's [some] cheese.
    Ima li sira? = Is there [any] cheese?)

I have/we have	Imam/imamo
You have/he (she, it) has	Imate/ima
I (we, etc) don't have	Nemam, nemamo etc
There is/isn't	Ima/nema
Toilet	Toalet, zavod
(pronounced as French "toilettes")	
Women/ladies	Žene/ženski
Men/Gentlemen	Muškarci/muški
Occupied	Zauzet
Vacant (free)	Slobodan
Open	Otvoren
Closed	Zatvoren
Here	Ovdje
There	Tamo
Left	Ljevo
Right	Desno
(Just, only) straight on	(Samo) ravno/pravo
Church	Crkva
Museum	Muzej
Palace (or mansion)	Dvor
Shop	Trgovina
Office	Ured/kancelarija

Postage stamp	Poštanska marka
Letter	Pismo
(By) airmail	Avionom
Money (in general)	Novac
Traveller's cheque	Putni ček
Exchange office	Mjenjačnica
(Numerals) One, two, etc	Jedan, dva, tri, četiri, pet, šest
sedam, osam, devet, deset.	
Eleven, twelve, etc	Jednaest, dvanaest, trinaest,
četrnaest, petnaest, šesnaest, sedamnaest, osamnaest, devetnaest.	
Twenty, thirty, etc	Dvadeset, trideset, četrdeset, pedeset,
šezdeset, sedamdeset, osamdeset, devedeset	
Hundred, two hundred	Sto, dvije stotine
Thousand, two thousand	Hiljada, dvije hiljade
First, second	Prvi, drugi
Third, fourth, fifth	Treći, četvrti, peti
And, or, but, also	i, ili, ali, takodjer
Dining room, restaurant	Restoran
Entrance, exit	Ulaz, izlaz
Inn, café	Gostiona, konoba, bife
Menu (bill of fare)	Meni, jelovik
Bill (account)	Račun
Receipt	Potvrda
Breakfast	Doručak
Lunch	Ručak
Dinner (in evening)	Večera
Soup	Juha
Starters	Predjelo
Fish	Riba
Meat	Meso
Eggs	Jaja
Vegetables	Povrće
Salad	Salata
Fruit	Voće
Cheese	Sir
Bread	Kruh, hleb
Ice cream	Sladoled
Coffee, tea	Kava, čaj
Beer, spirits	Pivo, rakija
(Red, white) wine	(Crno, bijelo) vino
(Mineral) water	Mineralna voda
(Fruit) juice	Sok
Cheers!	Živeli!
Good, bad	Dobar, loš
Big, little	Veli, mali
(Too) expensive	(Pre) skup
(Fairly) cheap	(Dosta) jeftin

A lot, a little, very	Mnogo, malo, vrlo
More	Više, još
Enough, too much	Dosta, previše
Passport	Pasoš
Customs	Carina
Timetable	Vozni red
Railway, bus (coach)	Željeznica, autobus
Bus station	Autobusni kolodvor
Bus stop	Autobusna stanica
Railway station	Željeznički kolodvor
Platform	Peron
Harbour, quay	Luka, kej
Boat, ship	Barka, brod
Ferry	Feri (or ferry)
Car ferry	Trajekt
Airport	Aerodrom
(Return) ticket	(Povratna) karta
Price	Cijena
Reservation	Rezervacija
Seat	Mjesto
First (second) class	Prva (druga) klasa
Waiting room	Čekaonica
To travel (by train, boat, bus, plane, car)	Putovati (vlakom, brodom, autobusom, avionom, autom)
Near, far	Blizu, daleko
To, from, towards	Do, od, za
Between, behind	Izmedju, ispred
Quickly, slowly	Brzo, polako
Yesterday, today	Jučer, danas
(Day after) tomorrow	(Preko)sutra
(Week) day	(Radni) dan
Every day	Svaki dan
Morning, evening, night	Jutro, večer, noć
Minute, hour(s)	Minuta, sat(i)
Half (quarter)-hour	Pola (četvrta) sata
One, two, three o'clock	Jedan, dva, tri sata
Half past four	pola pet, četiri i po
Quarter past three	tri i četvrt, tri i petnaest
Twenty to five	dvadeset do pet
Soon, later, now	Uskoro, kasnije, sada
(Days of the week)	Ponedeljak, utorak, srijeda, četrvrtak, petak, subora, nedelja (Sunday)
(Months)	januar, februar, mart, april, maj, juni, juli, august, septembar, oktobar, novembar, decembar
Help, police	Pomoć, milicija

143

Doctor, ambulance	Doktor, ambulanta
First aid	Prva pomoć
Pain, hospital	Bol, bolnica
Temperature	Temperatura
Vomiting, diarrhoea	Povraćanje, proljev

A glance at grammar

It's not possible to give even a bare outline of Serbo-Croat grammar here. All Slav languages (Russian, Polish, Czech, etc as well as Serbo-Croat) behave very differently from Indo-European tongues (Latin, German, English, French, etc). They are however "inflected" like Latin. That means that the endings of words vary according to what they're doing in a sentence. Split is the town. "In Split" becomes *u Splitu*. Verbs have different forms to indicate I, you, he, etc without using the pronouns we need. For instance, I have, you (singular) have, he/she/it has; we have, you (plural) have, they have is represented by the single words *imam, imaš, ima; imamo, imate, imaju.*

Latin and some modern Indo-European languages do much the same. But the Slav languages vary considerably by using separate verbs to indicate continuous instead of one-off action, by using their word-endings, and also their verb tenses, in somewhat different ways, and by treating numerals in particular very differently from West European languages.

They also differ in having no words for "the" and "a". If a Yugoslav says: "Would you like one glass of wine" he's not trying to limit your drinking. He just doesn't distinguish "a" glass from "one" glass. His language says simply "glass".